H. L. James'

Revised and expanded second edition

RUGS & POSTS

*The Story of Navajo Weaving
and Indian Trading*

Schiffer Publishing Ltd

4880 Lower Valley Road, Atglen, PA 19310

Dedication

To my wife, Mary Beth

Monument Valley, 1972

Library of Congress Cataloging-in-Publication Data

James. H.L. (Harold L.), 1933-
  (Rugs and posts)
  H.L. James' rugs and posts: the story of Navajo weaving and
Indian trading.--Rev. and expanded 2nd ed.
    p. cm.
  Includes bibliographical references.
  ISBN 0-7643-0808-4 (pbk.)
  1. Navajo textile fabrics. 2. Trading posts--Arizona. 3. Trading
posts--Southwest, New. I. Title.
E99.N3J36   1999
746.7'2--dc21   98-56524
                                          CIP

Revised in 1999.

Designed by "Sue"
Type set in Aldine 721 BT bolded/Aldine 721 Lt BT

ISBN: 0-7643-0808-4
Printed in China
1 2 3 4

Front Cover: Shiprock, northwestern New Mexico by H. L. James.
Back Cover: Sunrise Springs Trading Post, 1934, courtesy of
    National Park Service.
Frontispiece: *Monogram Pictorial* (15" X 16")
Weaver: Unknown
Source: Author's collection (1981)
Construction: Synthetic-dyed figures and designs, some minor
    commercial yarn in outlines, natural carded gray, mostly
    handspun.
Title Page Sketch: Shonto Trading Post, circa 1930, by Diane
    Nugent.

Published by Schiffer Publishing Ltd.
4880 Lower Valley Road
Atglen, PA 19310
Phone: (610) 593-1777; Fax: (610) 593-2002
E-mail: Schifferbk@aol.com
Please visit our web site catalog at www.schifferbooks.com
Please write for a free catalog.
This book may be purchased from the publisher.
Please include $3.95 for shipping.

In Europe, Schiffer books are distributed by
Bushwood Books
6 Marksbury Rd.
Kew Gardens
Surrey TW9 4JF England
Phone: 44 (0)181 392-8585; Fax: 44 (0)181 392-9876
E-mail: Bushwd@aol.com

Please try your bookstore first.

We are interested in hearing from authors
with book ideas on related subjects.

CONTENTS

PREFACE TO THE REVISED EDITION

In late February 1997, a small band of Navajos (called Mustangs) swept south from Monument Valley into the desert and defeated a similar size force from Blue Ridge to capture the Class 3-A State Basketball Championship of Arizona.

It has been ten years since *Rugs and Posts* was first published and during that short length of time, it is remarkable to see the economic and social strides made on the Navajo Reservation. Goods and services have increased and significant gains have been made in cultural awareness, education, medical care, transportation and employment practices.

Historically, there is some sadness to all of this advancement. For the most part, the term "trader" is actually a misnomer and the old trading post days have fallen by the wayside. Yet, at least for a short time longer, one can still feel the ambiance of a traditional reservation trading post at Two Grey Hills to the east and Shonto on the west. Gratefully, the foresight of the National Park Service in acquiring the Hubbell complex at Ganado will always ensure a glimpse into this storied era.

In 1934, Charles Avery Amsden predicted: *The demise of Navajo weaving will ultimately be won by the Americanization of the weaver* — perhaps, but not at this point in time. Rug production is high, the quality is excellent and prices are soaring. New style innovations are taking place and three-ply, pastel-colored yarns are being exclusively developed and manufactured for Navajo weavers. A return to traditional patterns has found recent popularity, such as a revival in Late Classic Period broadbanded motifs and Transition Period Germantown "eyedazzlers." It appears that a renaissance occurs in Navajo weaving every twenty years or so — just in time to rescue itself from a questionable future. Today, the skilled weaver is regarded as a true artisan and the results of their efforts are finally becoming financially rewarding.

The revised edition of *Rugs and Posts* is an attempt to continue the chronicle of a creative people living in a remarkable land. This edition provides additional information on the history of the trading post system, including a short biographical sketch on C. N. Cotton, an individual who contributed greatly to the historical development of Navajo weaving. Also included are two appendices that outline the necessary steps in purchasing and caring for a Navajo rug. Prices have been brought up to date in a twenty-year (1978-1998) comparative chart to show that buying a Navajo rug is still a good investment. Although most of the trading posts, traders and weavers are no longer in place as per the 1988 edition, their names are retained here for their historical significance.

The revised edition could not have been completed without the assistance of the following persons: Les Wilson of Two Grey Hills, Bill Malone of Hubbell Trading Post, Bill Foutz of Shiprock, New Mexico and Bruce Burnham of Sanders, Arizona; to my wife, Mary Beth, for her editorial input, word processing and cheerful support and suggestions for the text. Additional information was provided by the Navajo Bureau of Vital Statistics, Window Rock, Arizona.

November, 1998
Seeley Lake, Montana

ACKNOWLEDGMENTS

This type of book preparation, whether in the field or at a desk, is more exciting than laborious, both from the sorting of gathered research and from the people that are met along the way. There are many who assisted, but I am particularly indebted to two long-time Gallup, New Mexico friends: librarian Octavia Fellin, and Martin Link, editor of *The Indian Trader*. After several years of being away from the Southwest, these two enthusiastic providers of information were my principal contacts and, as always, were very cooperative and dependable. To Bruce Burnham of Sanders, Arizona, and Bill Malone at Hubbell Trading Post, for freely sharing their knowledge and providing insights on the state of Navajo weaving and Indian trading as it exists today. To Sallie Wagner of Santa Fe, New Mexico and Fred Patton of Chinle, Arizona, for entrusting me with valuable photographs. And finally, to Shonto's Melissa Trolet, a little-known trader at a little-known place who, on that raw November day in 1987, offered a little-known writer a welcome hand and a gracious respite — truly a spirit in keeping with Indian tradership.

The art work in Chapter 2 was rendered by Hallmark artist Donald J. Mills of Evanston, Illinois. The title page sketch and layout/design consultations for the book are by Diane Nugent of Butte, Montana.

March 15, 1988
Butte, MT

Dineth and environs. *Courtesy of Katonah Gallery, Katonah, New York.*

Chapter 1

HISTORY

The People

They call themselves *Dine*, meaning simply "the people," and their homeland, *Dineth*. The word Navajo (Navaho) is of Tewa origin, which translates to "great planted fields." As determined from distributions of the Athapascan language, from which Navajo is derived, a nucleus of wandering clans crossed the Bering Strait about 3,000 years ago and moved gradually across what is presently southeastern Alaska and western Canada (Watson, 1973). Some anthropologists believe that a 700-year nomadic trek transpired that eventually led the Navajo and their kinsman, the Apache, into watersheds of the Chama and San Juan rivers some time around 1200-1400 A.D. Their exact route is uncertain, but logically the path of least resistance would lay along the eastern plains bordering the Rocky Mountains.

They had not made their presence felt by the year 1540, however, as chroniclers of Coronado's Expedition fail to mention them in their journals. The first known historical reference occurs in the *Relaciones* of Father Gerónimo Zárate de Salmerón, who wrote of their activities in the late 1500s. Fray Alonzo de Benavides also mentions them in 1630 as being good farmers.

Sometime during the mid-1600s, the Navajo culture, now well established and prosperous, began an altering expansion with the Apaches severing ties and traveling south into desert environs to form their own *Dineth*. The early Spanish explorers referred to these people as the "Apache de Navahu". Perhaps because of drought, or friction with nearby Pueblo centers, the Navajo clans moved west and south to occupy a general area surrounding the sanctuary of Canyon de Chelly.

The wheels of Spanish occupation were set in motion by the advance of Coronado in 1540, followed four decades later by colonizers and the clergy under Juan de Oñate. The Spanish brought with them herds of churro-type sheep and goats — hence the origin of wool preparation and weaving in the Southwest.

The possession of the Rio Grande region under Spanish rule brought conflict. The Pueblo Indians became subservient to the Europeans and suffered greatly by their dominance. This ultimately led to the Pueblo Revolt of 1680, whereby the Spanish were driven from the territory. Fearing reprisals, many Pueblo dwellers sought refuge and joined their neighbors to the west — hence the introduction of weaving skills to the Navajo.

Twelve years later in 1692, Diego de Vargas reclaimed Nuevo Mexico, and a relatively peaceful period followed for most of the 18th century, broken occasionally by assaults by Navajos to acquire livestock and goods. In turn, the Indians were becoming subjects of slave raids by the Spanish. In 1805, one such Spanish atrocity was the ruthless slaughter of over 100 elderly men, women and children huddled in a cave in a tributary of Canyon de Chelly. The place is now called Canyon del Muerto, Spanish for "Canyon of the Dead". Throughout the period the Navajos, now adept at their weaving skills, expanded their blanket trade network to include Plains Indians, as well as exchanges with the Spanish and the Pueblos.

Mexico gained its independence from Spain in 1821 and opened its boundaries to trade with the United States the following year with a warm reception of the first wagons over the Santa Fe Trail (James, 1966). This great commerce of the plains, which was to last in varying degrees until 1880, brought the Navajos a new source of supply in yarns, dyes and bolts of cloth in return for blankets that flowed into eager Anglo markets. A true cottage industry was now in place.

During Mexican rule (1821-1846), hostilities increased as slave raids were now initiated by both sides — the barter usually being for horses from neighboring tribes. This trafficking and plunder was, at the time of the American Acquisition in 1846, so prevalent that it ceased to be regarded as wrong. It was these unsettling attitudes that confronted the occupational Army of the West, and as General Stephen Watts Kearney declared himself a "protector" instead of a conqueror, the resident population sensed perhaps a deliverance from their greatest menace — the marauding Indian. On September 18, 1846, Kearney dispatched three companies of Missouri Volunteers under the command of Lt. Colonel Cosgreve Jackson to the remote mission village of Seboyeta located sixty miles west of Albuquerque. No name was given to this frontier outpost and the garrison which was stationed there functioned mainly as a show of strength. The Seboyeta guard failed to impress the Indians; incursions and depredations continued to increase. In the weeks that followed, the situation worsened to the point where Kearney was continually besieged with delegations from communities all demanding protection from the Navajo menace. A changed course of action appeared necessary.

In 1846, a treaty approach was attempted. Colonel Alexander W. Doniphan, representing General Kearney, met with Navajo chiefs on November 22nd at a noted rendezvous point in the northern foothills of the Zuni Mountains called *Shash 'B Tow* (Navajo for "Bear Springs"). In formal terms it was stated that the Navajos would swear allegiance with the Americans, and that all residents of the newly-acquired territory would be administered by the United States government. Further, it stipulated that the Indians would cease all warlike activities against the residents of New Mexico. Also included were provisions for full restoration of all stolen property and livestock, and the release of all Mexican captives. The Indians made their mark upon a treaty paper; however, their outward show of friendship and good will was misleading. Their animosities toward the Mexicans were too deeply seated to be simply dissolved by the signing of a document.

The Doniphan Treaty proved to be a failure. Furthermore, the presence of a foreign military power in their homeland served only to incite the Indians. During the years 1847-1850, incursions and hostilities reached enormous proportions. Fort Marcy at Santa Fe became nothing more than a huge staging area for outfitting expeditions into Navajoland. More treaties were signed, more treaties were broken. Several peace negotiations failed even before the treaty expedition had returned to Santa Fe. It became an endless, frustrating game to which a solution seemed impossible.

On July 19, 1851, a soldier of considerable experience, Colonel Edwin Vose Sumner, assumed command of the Ninth Military Department of New Mexico. He immediately undertook to revolutionize the whole system of frontier defense. He authorized a site for the erection of Fort Union (60 miles east of Santa Fe) to serve as departmental headquarters, replacing Fort Marcy. He withdrew the garrison from the Seboyeta outpost and on September 18, 1851, issued general orders for the construction of still another post to be located along the east front of the Defiance Mountains. The site chosen was at a Navajo shrine called *Tse Hot' Sohih* (Navajo meaning

"Meadows Between the Rocks"). The post was designed to house five companies and was appropriately named Fort Defiance.

Colonel Sumner, with his sometimes criticized reorganization, had the desired effect upon the Navajo — peace. To assure a lasting friendship, he instituted commercial trade with the Indians. He directed the distribution of quartermaster stores to supplement their needs during severe winters. He provided technical services and agricultural aids. His assistance reached into tribal government where he preached the advantages of affairs conducted in a democratic manner.

Fort Defiance remained the great fortress of peace for nearly eight years. Several violations of theft and murder did occur but the incidents were tactfully handled without provocation for war.

By the late 1850s the Indians became restless. This uneasiness grew from the reservation treaties of Meriwether (1855) and Bonneville (1858), in which the Navajos were geographically restricted within specified boundary lines. These limits were defined by the San Juan River on the north, to the Zuni River on the south at a point just east of Zuni Pueblo. The western boundary was placed along a line running south from the San Juan River (north of present Kayenta), to the confluence of Chevalon Creek and the Little Colorado River between present-day Holbrook and Winslow in Arizona. The eastern boundary forbade all Indian claims east of Chaco Canyon in New Mexico. These treaties, although specifying their traditional lands, restricted their travel outside of the set boundaries. In short, the Navajos felt like prisoners in their own domain.

The strict conformity to reservation life, coupled with severe winters, forced many Navajos upon the plunder trail. A breach began to widen. Minor incidents became major incidents; plots were instigated. Finally, on the morning of April 30, 1860, the peace was broken. With the shouts of an estimated 1,000 warriors, Fort Defiance was attacked. The fort sustained itself for the entire day. Only when darkness made it difficult to distinguish friend from foe, did the Indians withdraw into the surrounding hills.

The brazen attack upon Fort Defiance threw New Mexico back into the grip of another Indian war. Additional troops of calvary reinforced the red-rock perimeters. Another post was established (August 31, 1860) on the grounds of the old Doniphan Treaty site at Bear Springs. It was named for the presiding Department Commander, Colonel Thomas Turner ("Little Lord") Fauntleroy. Throughout the remainder of 1860 and the early part of 1861, the United States Army became engaged in a full-scale Indian campaign, the likes of which the territory had never before witnessed.

In the spring of 1861, the Military Department of New Mexico faced still another peril, brought about by the secession of Southern states, and the apparent Confederate plan to invade the desert Southwest. To meet

Fort Defiance, circa 1855. *Courtesy of Museum of New Mexico.*

Western military installations. Department of New Mexico, 1846-1868.

this threatened invasion of the territory, the newly appointed Department Commander, Colonel Edward S. Canby, set the Indian problem aside and began concentrating his defenses closer to the Rio Grande. Fort Defiance was abandoned on April 25th, its garrison transferred to Fort Fauntleroy.

By the summer of 1861, the impending Confederate threat became a reality. On July 27th, Lt. Colonel John R. Baylor (C.S.A.) struck north from El Paso and captured Fort Fillmore (south of present-day Las Cruces). Baylor declared that all of New Mexico below Socorro to be Confederate territory, designating Mesilla as its capital.

On September 28, 1861, a general order of the U.S. Department of the Army changed the name of Fort Fauntleroy to Fort Lyon when Colonel Fauntleroy resigned his commission to join the Confederacy. The post's new name honored General Nathaniel Lyon who had been killed weeks earlier at the Battle of Wilson Creek, Missouri. Three months later on December 10th, Fort Lyon was abandoned and the garrison was used to strengthen the force at Fort Craig below Socorro.

On February 14, 1862, the Texas Army (C.S.A.), under the command of General Henry H. Sibley (who had replaced Colonel Baylor), began its tidal march up the Rio Grande. It defeated the Union forces at Fort Craig in the historic Battle of Valverde on February 21st. Continuing intact, General Sibley's army engulfed Albuquerque on March 2nd and Santa Fe on March 23rd. Their dreams of conquest were shattered, however, when they were badly defeated by Union troops, reinforced by Colorado Volunteers, at the Battle of Glorieta Pass (southeast of Santa Fe) on March 26th and 28th.

The Indians had taken full advantage of the military turmoil created by the Confederate invasion, and their raids greatly increased during this period. In the summer of 1862, the new military commander for New Mexico, General James H. Carleton, turned his full attention to the Navajo. His plans for the complete submission of the tribe called for a "roundup" and the placing of the Indians on a supervised military reservation; the philosophy being, "it is cheaper to feed them than to fight them". His "Indian policy" also included the authorization of a new post to be built on the eastern slopes of the Zuni Mountains to serve as staging area for his plan. General Carleton named the new post Fort Wingate to honor Captain Benjamin A. Wingate, an infantry officer who had served at Fort Lyon, and who had died of wounds during heroic conduct in the Battle of Valverde (James, 1967).

The site chosen for the fort was at Ojo de Gallo (Spanish for "Chicken Spring") south of present-day Grants, New Mexico. Construction began on September 30, 1862. The actual erection of permanent buildings was a slow process, as materials were salvaged and hauled by wagon

from old Fort Lyon 45 miles to the west. The fort was formally commissioned on October 22, 1862.

On November 9, 1862, Carleton notified the War Department of the establishment of still another post, to be named Fort Sumner in honor of the old campaigner of the 1850s, Edwin Vose Sumner. The fort was located 165 miles southeast of Santa Fe at a point on the east side of the Rio Pecos known as Bosque Redondo (Spanish for "Round Grove"). This post would supervise Carleton's internment camp of the Navajos.

By the spring of 1863, Fort Wingate was beginning to take shape. Four companies of the Fourth New Mexico Mounted Rifles and one company of California Volunteers, under the command of Lt. Colonel Jose Francisco Chavez, had taken up quarters. In addition to these troops the garrison was further strengthened by Colonel Christopher "Kit" Carson's E, F and H companies of the First New Mexico Volunteers — a force of 736 men (Fontana, 1988).

Carleton was now ready to take the field against the Navajo. In his first movement, on July 28, 1863, he directed Carson to set up a base of operations at the ruins of old Fort Defiance (renamed Fort Canby). He then sent word to all Indian leaders that total war was to commence, and that any Navajo not wishing to engage in these hostilities could surrender at either Fort Wingate or Fort Canby. Some Indians, observing the strength building of the "blue coats", and the proclamation of a vigorous war, began surrendering in small groups. By fall the count was 180 tribesmen, a number quite short of Carleton's idea of total suppression.

In mid-October 1863, Carleton released the full fury of his "Indian policy". He undertook a scorched-earth campaign, the likes of which the Indians had never imagined. Carson's troops pursued them night and day, week after week, over mesas, mountains, and deserts, and through drifts of winter snows. The military pursuit included the needless destruction of planting fields and grain storages, the burning of hogans and orchards, and the wanton slaughter of sheep and cattle. By the end of 1863, the Navajos found themselves in a desperate state. To worsen matters, they lay in the grip of a severe winter, faced with complete extermination, not only by the saber but from exposure and hunger. On January 12, 1864, Carson delivered the final blow by attacking their only remaining stronghold — Canyon de Chelly. There, huddled together, demoralized, too weak to resist, the once proud lords of the canyonlands submitted to the will of the white man.

On March 4, 1864, more than two thousand Navajos filed out of Fort Canby and began the infamous trek to Fort Sumner, that is known in history today as the "Long Walk" — a 350-mile journey to the Rio Pecos. The route soon displayed a stream of ragged humanity that continued throughout 1864. The pathway was marked by the remains of many Indians who crawled to the wayside to die a lingering death brought about by dysentery and exposure.

Carleton had envisioned his 40-square-mile reservation to be a self-supporting agricultural system, but the 6,000 acres set aside for tilling were found to be impregnated with alkali and, as a consequence, the yield of crops was low. By the beginning of 1865, the population had grown in excess of 9,000, which included some 400 renegade Apaches transferred from Fort Stanton in southern New Mexico. The large population, coupled with the first years crop failure, began to tax the army's quartermaster in its quest for food.

From the beginning, the troubles at Bosque Redondo were compounded by dissension and internal disorders. Conflicts broke out between Navajos and Apaches, Indian agents and the military, and between civil authorities and the military. Inadequate food and clothing was a prime complaint. The confined were undernourished and plagued by disease. The brackish water from the river resulted in mass dysentery. Desertions and "runaways" were frequent. Added to this, prisoners in unprotected sectors became the targets of bands of Comanches and Kiowas who roamed the vast Llano Estacado to the east.

Bosque Redondo became nothing more than a huge concentration camp without regard to the preservation of human life. It soon fell under attack by civic leaders of the territory, who demanded a complete investigation of conditions. The tremendous expenditure necessary to maintain the compound was also questioned and criticized. Finally, the shameful disgrace of the encampment reflected on the people of the territory and aroused political feelings to the point where candidates and parties were labeled either "pro-Bosque" or "anti-Bosque". Editorials were demanding the resignation of General Carleton.

The plight of the Navajos began attracting national attention that could no longer be ignored. On March 3, 1865, a Joint Special Committee composed of members of both houses of Congress was appointed to investigate conditions along the Rio Pecos. The committee, headed by chairman James R. Doolittle of Wisconsin, personally inspected Bosque Redondo during the month of July. Their findings resulted in a report which recommended that the care of the Indians be transferred from military control to one of civil authority, namely the Department of the Interior.

Charges and counter charges were hurled in both directions over the report. In early 1866, the Territorial Assembly in Santa Fe joined the controversy by publicly condemning Carleton's "Indian policy". They adopted a resolution which was personally forwarded to President Andrew Johnson, urging the removal of the department commander. After much debate, the government slowly began to grind out a solution.

Finally, on September 19, 1866, the first steps were taken. General James H. Carleton was relieved of his position and replaced by General G.W. Getty. On December 31st the control of the Indians was transferred to the

Bosque Redondo, 1866.
Navajos under guard at the internment camp at Fort Sumner, New Mexico. Late Classic Period shoulder wraps designed with broad stripes and bands are much in evidence. *Photo courtesy of Museum of New Mexico.*

Bureau of Indian Affairs under the Department of Interior. The military was instructed to give assistance in Indian problems only when requested by the commissioner.

The Secretary of Interior and the Commissioner of Indian Affairs, with the authority delegated by Congress, entertained the proposition of returning the Navajos to their homeland. The Interior Department appointed a committee to survey the resources of their original reservation in hopes of relocating them back on their native soil. When all reports were favorably accepted, a Peace Commission, headed by Lt. General William Tecumseh Sherman, was selected to negotiate a treaty. Sherman arrived at Fort Sumner on May 28, 1867. Three days later a treaty was drafted and accepted by the dejected Indians. They were now allowed to reverse the "Long Walk," and at sunrise on the morning of June 18, 1868, a column of Indians, which reportedly stretched for 10 miles, began the return to their beloved redrocks and their ravaged homeland.[1]

The Navajos called their time at Bosque Redondo, *nabondzod*, "the fearing time" (Utley and Washburn, 1977). If that period on the Rio Pecos seemed dreadful, what lay ahead during the early days of resettlement was not much better. As specified by the treaty, the Indians were to receive food, clothing, tools and supplies, and education for their children for a period of ten years. In the fall of 1869, more than 9,000 Navajos gathered at Fort Defiance for a sheep distribution allotment that consisted of two animals for every man, woman and child (Koenig and Koeing, 1986). The economic and social dependency of the Fort Defiance "ration days", and government reliance that has prevailed into the modern era, have been inextricably linked ever since.

Fort Defiance ration days, circa 1870.
Courtesy of Smithsonian Institution

The Traders

The involvement of the federal government to regulate commerce with Indian tribes dates back to April 18, 1796, when President George Washington signed a bill to establish trading houses to serve various southern and western Indian nations. This was followed on June 30, 1835, by an Act of Congress to Regulate Trade and Intercourse with Indian tribes of the Southwest.

The early Indian traders were a rugged phenom and functioned in an independent lifestyle that required endurance, perseverance and a dash of ingenuity; a "woolly lot", if you will, with a keen sense for the slightest margin for profit. They spawned from that breed of French trappers in the southern Rockies to Comancheros who bartered their questionable inventories from the packs of wandering caravans on the Great Plains.

The first Navajo trader who operated from a fixed location was George A. Richardson, who was licensed on October 26, 1865, to administer the store at Bosque Redondo. Later, other licenses were issued at the camp to Joseph A. LaRue, Oscar M. Brown and W.W. Martin.[2]

The "true" trading post evolved when the Navajos were released to the guardianship of the Bureau of Indian Affairs at Fort Defiance. Authorized by Congress, the Commissioner now had the sole power to license and appoint traders. The Fort Defiance traders were: Lehman Spiegelberg of Santa Fe, who was licensed on August 28, 1868, Cole F. Ludlove of Valencia County, New Mexico (October 1868), and John Ayres of Abuquiu, New Mexico (1870), followed by his brother Lionel in 1872.

As the Indians slowly disseminated throughout the remote recesses of their homeland, so did the trading post. As these "general stores" sprang up, a unique entrepreneurial institution began to emerge — headed by a middleman who served two worlds of exchange: flour, coffee, canned goods, tools and clothing in return for woven products, wool, sheep, hides, and in good years, piñon nuts.[3]

Every person who traded on the Navajo Reservation did so with government approval — revocable at any time. The rules were strict, although not always enforceable. A bond of $10,000 was required up front and issued only to U.S. citizens who could demonstrate exceptional character and satisfactory references. The trader was responsible for the conduct of his employees. They were also held accountable for price lists and monthly invoices, which were audited by the Bureau. Articles of merchandise were fixed by said office and the allowable return of profit at any time could not exceed 25 percent of the cost of the goods, plus freight (Commissioner of Indian Affairs Annual Report, 1886). The sale of ammunition, firearms and alcoholic beverages were definitely prohibited, however, off-reservation outlets and nearby towns were available for such purchases.

The prerequisites of successful trading usually included a favorable location (with water), such as at a point where established travel routes existed, or in an area where several clans might settle. This would ensure a population base upon which to build a reliable clientele. Learning the difficult Navajo language was a must; establishing some early rapport with headsmen was tactful; a willingness to extend reasonable credit (pawn) showed business sense; and of course, marrying a "local girl" couldn't hurt — several did. If a new trader was resourceful, he would soon begin working with area weavers by suggesting certain dyes and designs, and in return paying a top price for the best products.[4]

The early facilities were crude — nothing more than tents or adobe (mud) huts. Since land ownership was prohibited, most traders never considered equity or home improvements a very high priority, therefore, the posts were usually of modest means and costs, if not primitive in some cases.[5]

If the site was in or near a mountain locale, the post construction was of logs; in desert valleys it was usually of sandstone slabs cemented with mud. The store was often small with living quarters in the back. Space was limited, particularly when the place also served as a social center for the exchange of news. The atmosphere of the trading post, with its seemingly endless array of colorful labeled goods and modern implements, was awesome to the Navajo and might be compared to what a major shopping mall would be to the present-day urbanite. The front door opened into a sort of compound called a "bullpen" — a corral-type enclosure bounded by high counters on three sides. A pot-bellied stove usually occupied the center floor plan with wooden benches outlining the perimeter. McNitt (1962, p.75) best describes the scene:

Shelves behind the high counters, therefore, were loaded to ceiling level: groceries on this side, dry goods on that side. Still there was not enough room to display everything, and so the roof beams dripped merchandise as a cave roof collects stalactites. From hooks and nails dangled Dutch ovens and frying pans of dull black iron, glinting oil lanterns, and hardware — tin pots and kettles and washtubs — coils of yellow rope, bridles, saddles, and tanned deer hides or skins of mountain lions. The smell of the post always was the same, desert or mountain: a concentrated essence of very dry dust, of sweet tanned leather and sour sweat and oil and metal, an abrasive lining of spit, tobacco smoke, and kerosene, and sometimes, for charity's sake, a whiff of sagebrush carried through the chinks and cracks of walls and roof. *Reproduced from* The Indian Traders *(McNitt, 1962), courtesy University of Oklahoma Press*

Arbuckles Coffee — the staple of common ground. Perhaps no other single product confirmed more deals, established friendships, or bonded two races of people than "Hosteen Cohay." A favorite of the Navajo, the Ariosa brew played an important role in reservation life. The wooden shipping crates provided materials for infant cradle boards, repair of post walls, gates and corrals, use in store counters and shelving and the building of sheds, privies and outbuildings. Even the one-pound paper packaging was imprinted with various prize signatures, which could be redeemed for a penny or a stick of candy. *Photo courtesy of National Park Service.*

Sunrise Springs Trading Post, 1934 (left, Clarence A. Wheeler and Albert Hugh Lee). *Courtesy of National Park Service.*

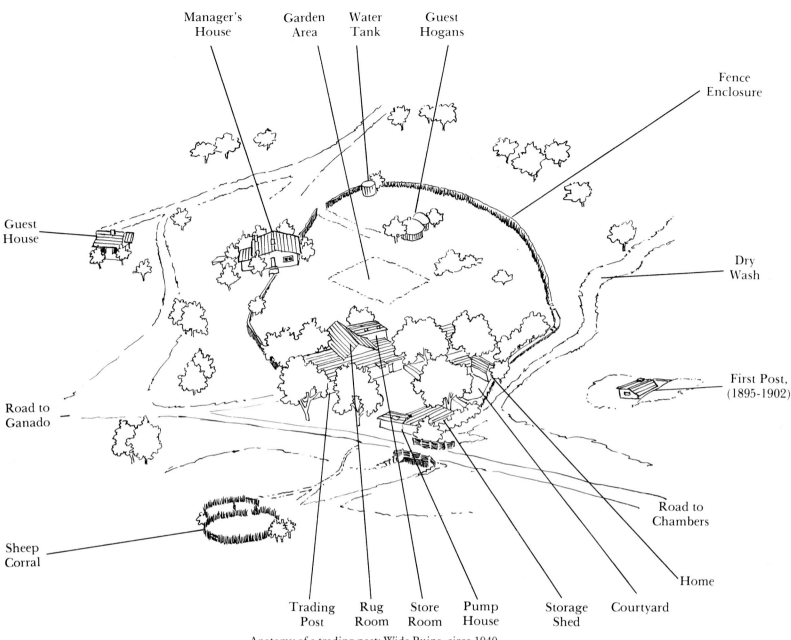

Manager's House · Garden Area · Water Tank · Guest Hogans · Fence Enclosure · Guest House · Dry Wash · Road to Ganado · First Post, (1895-1902) · Sheep Corral · Road to Chambers · Home · Trading Post · Rug Room · Store Room · Pump House · Storage Shed · Courtyard

Anatomy of a trading post: Wide Ruins, circa 1940.

If business prospered and the trader felt acceptance in his chosen role, some expansion was in order, and soon the place would take on the appearance of a small settlement. In time, a warehouse, barn, corrals and various outbuildings were added. At some places, a guest hogan was constructed nearby.[6]

Loneliness was one major obstacle to cope with, particularly if a post was located in a remote area. Traders who were single, without any family or hired help, could find themselves in a desperate state of solitude at times. More often it was in the winter when deep snows inhibited even horse traffic, causing days, even weeks to pass without contact with another person. Some traders became "spooked" with this aspect of the business and several left the reservation for more personable endeavors.

With the advent of tourism in the early part of the 20th century, the trader found a new source of revenue — the sightseeing Anglo. To serve these dauntless travelers, the trading post also became a retail outlet for rugs,

as well as providing food, supplies, and another duty to tend to — pumping gas. With all variables now in place, these remote havens functioned as an integral component of consumer economy on the reservation and became indispensable emporiums for goods and services.

The trader became the main link between the Anglo world and the remote civilization of the reservation Indian. Other than the daily responsibilities of store keeping, he acted as their spokesman beyond the boundaries of their world. Displaying compassion and sensitivity, he lent an understanding ear and served as their benefactor, counselor and protector. He advised in medical and legal matters, mediated disputes, assisted in chores, helped bury their dead, marketed their goods, and in the process became loved and respected by all that he attended. As trust was garnered, he became highly influential in his trade area.

In 1868, the initial three licenses that were granted to commence trade with the Navajos was doubled by 1877.

At the turn of the century there were 36, and in 1943, the heyday of the Navajo trader, there were 95 government-licensed posts on the reservation, with an additional 50 or more operating outside the boundaries (Ledger of Licensed Indian Traders, U.S. National Archives, Washington, D.C., n.d.). The posts have been declining in number ever since.

Following World War II, attitudes changed on the reservation. Nearly 3,000 returning Navajo servicemen and women, now armed with knowledge of other people, other lands and other ways, had increased their awareness of broader values — employment, education and a desire to enter the mainstream of the outside world. With this changing philosophy, the *naalye he bahoogan* (the trading post), no longer became the center of their cultural existence and, although continuing as a supplier of goods and a center for marketing, its role as a dominant societal influence was beginning to diminish.

New trends continue to sweep the reservation, and in the modern era it is forcing the old-time trader into the twilight of his time. The trading post developed as a result of isolation and bad roads. Where wagon ruts and sheep trails once wandered, there are now seemingly endless stretches of asphalt highways. When once it took days to haul trade goods from the railhead, they are now delivered in hours — in refrigerated carriers, no less. The traditional patterns of the past are now being replaced by modern conveniences—a paradox of weighing the values of an existence in a primitive land, but exercising the choice of purchasing assorted frozen dinners and a good selection of video tapes.

Since 1980, over half of the active trading posts operating at that time have either been abandoned, razed, lost leases, or have been purchased by a convenience store chain. Trade centers such as Chinle, the very core of Navajo tradition, no longer supports a true trader. Place names synonymous with rug styles like Wide Ruins, Burnt Water and Crystal no longer exist. Others are destined for change and perhaps before the end of this century, the last trader will become inundated beneath the "wave of progress", thus ending a 130-year era of remarkable coexistence with a red brethren in a red land.

Epilogue

The day is not too far off when the [tribal] council will allow all sorts of businesses to operate on the reservation, and this will mark the end of the old Indian trader.
Roman Hubbell, 1948
Gallup Independent

The Craft

Much has been written on the history of Navajo weaving. It is generally agreed that the events of the craft are categorized into six periods of development: Classic Period (1700-1850), Late Classic Period (1850-1863), Transition Period (1868-1890), Rug Period (1890-1930), Revival Period (1930-1940) and the Regional Style Period (1940-present).

Classic Period (1700-1850) — The Navajos learned the art of weaving on upright looms (as opposed to Hispanic

Tourists — Bless Them! *Photo courtesy of Museum of New Mexico.*

horizontal looms) from Pueblo Indians who fled into Navajo sanctuaries following the revolt of 1680, although some cotton weaving may have been gleaned from them somewhat earlier in that century.[7] Crude clothing was the main objective: dresses, shirts and breech cloths, shoulder blankets, leggings, belts, hair cords and ponchos.

The earliest surviving examples from Massacre Cave (1805) show that patterns were simple, primarily in narrow stripes and bands. Colors were mostly the natural wool tones of white, gray, brown, tan and black. Some vegetal dying was used in ranges of rust, yellow and green. Indigo blue was introduced early by the Spanish and became widely used throughout the period.

Some trade in blankets with the Spanish began on a small scale in the 1700s, as well as with other Pueblo neighbors. During the latter part of the period, Spanish enslavement of some Navajos resulted in the first definitive style piece, the so-called "slave blanket". In the 1800s, woven Mexican-Saltillo serapes were finding their way into markets in the upper Rio Grande region. These products would soon influence and inspire Navajo weavers into design adaptations, particularly the diamond and broad, wavy band motifs.

Late Classic Period (1850-1863) — In the 150 years or so after they began weaving, the Navajo far surpassed their Pueblo teachers as weavers and suppliers of blankets for the Spanish, other Indian tribes, and by 1850, to American soldiers and settlers. The period brought the weavers increasing economic success. The popular shoulder wrap for men, distinctively patterned in broad black, blue (indigo) and white horizontal bands, was termed the *Chief Blanket*.[8] This widely sought after fabric was later modified to incorporate red bayeta threads with design alterations of diamonds, boxes, crosses and stripes. The blanket was very popular among other Indian tribes and U.S. military leaders.

The serape and the poncho serape were also major period pieces. The latter woven longer than wide, and with a slit for the head, was draped over the wearer's body to form a front and back. Most serapes were fashioned in Mexican-Saltillo designs of serrated diamonds and broad wavy bands. Woven on horizontal looms, the Mexican pieces were usually constructed in half panels, and then sewn together to fashion the full fabric.

Experimentation in design and pattern highlighted the Late Classic Period, along with a greater technical excellence in spinning and weaving. Unable to produce brilliant red, the Navajo traded for bolts of English manufactured baize (a wool cloth called bayeta in Spanish).[9] The weavers unraveled the red fabric, respun the threads and used them in combinations with native wool. American flannel, when available, was similarly used. Additional imports into the Southwest, through Spain, Mexico and United States frontier routes, were the pre-aniline, three-ply European yarns, called Saxony. The combina-

tion of bayeta red and indigo blue, used with the distinctive sheens of Saxony, yielded highly marketable items. With new colors came inventiveness in design, such as terraced motifs, zigzags, diamonds and outlined crosses.

By the early 1860s the golden age of weaving had arrived, but at its seemingly grandest hour, the textile revolution of the period tragically collapsed with the fall and imprisonment of the Navajo people.

Deprived of natural wool while in exile, weavers turned to machine-made yarn supplied by their captors and continued to make blankets for sale.

Transition Period (1868-1890) — With their pacification, the Navajos were allowed to return to their beloved redrocks. Now faced with the task of rebuilding their sheep flocks and wool supply, the freed weavers, becoming familiar with commercial yarn, slowly began to embark on a wild extravaganza of color. Bayeta and Saxony wools of the Late Classic Period were replaced in the early 1870s by a newly introduced yarn called Germantown. This was a coarse, four-ply and three-ply, aniline-dyed yarn, much of it manufactured in western Pennsylvania. At the height of Germantown use (1890) came a period of decline; design carelessness and gaudy color balances became the rule.[10] The commercial aspects of the craft became misdirected and drifted into confusion.

Sharing the period of resettlement with the Navajo was a new breed of man, the Indian trader, a unique type of individual who bridged the great gap between the red and white races. By the late 1870s, government-licensed traders were spreading across the reservation, setting up remote outposts of goods and personally concerning themselves with the promotion of weaving. The imagination of the trader brought new stimulus to the craft. Goods sold by traders introduced the weavers to a new field of visual designs: the alphabet, patterns on supply sacks, pictures and catalogs.

As the 20th century approached, the weaving industry slowly regained its balance. There were two main reasons for this change: (1) the trader and the development of regional styles of weaving and (2) the transition from blanket to rug. Rugs were created when weavers stopped making blankets for themselves, turning instead to another trader-provided item, the machine-made Pendleton blanket, as wearing apparel. The result was a new-found market for heavier and larger weaves, supplying the white man with floor coverings. Commercial Germantown yarns generally lost favor with traders, and weavers turned again to using handspun wool.

Rug Period (1890-1930) — Already in use by the 1880s, commercial dyes (now available in individual color packets) were gaining favor on the reservation, and the new colors gave greater intensity to the fine textiles that were being produced.[11] New styles were experimented with, one of the most significant being the bordered rug. The

Chief Blanket, circa 1865.

Germantown "eyedazzler," circa 1878.

Cayatanito, 1874. *Courtesy of Smithsonian Institution.*

Rugs reproduced from Hollister, 1903. *Courtesy of Gallup, New Mexico Public Library.*

Ganado, circa 1891.

Bayeta, circa 1840.

framed format was encouraged by traders for its appeal to eastern clientele. By 1920, few rugs left the loom without some form of outside band to enclose the pattern.[12]

By the early 1900s came the greatest rug market the industry had yet known, and production was soon pressed to keep up with demand. The greatest stimuli was an increasing awareness of the Native American culture. Informational outgrowths from archaeological expeditions, Indian fairs, inter-tribal ceremonials, curio outlets, art, photography and publications all benefited the Navajo marketplace.

With improved rail transportation and back roads, there appeared a new singular force — "the tourist", an intrepid soul with laced-up boots, camera in hand and money for the purchase of crafts. Fulfilling dreams of exploration in aboriginal America they came in droves, many rocking along on a train whose very name stirred excitement — "The Santa Fe Chief". They caravaned in canvas-topped Buicks and touring Packards — all in search of wondrous places, and in the process, purchased thousands of Navajo rugs as evidence of their adventure.

The Fred Harvey Company, under the aegis of the Santa Fe Railroad, developed a popular sightseeing concession called *Indian Detours*. From a headquarters at the La Fonda Hotel in Santa Fe, Hunter Clarkston managed a personalized service which featured "Harveycars", complete with picnic hampers, drivers dressed in Western outfits and tour hostesses adorned in velveteen blouses and turquoise jewelry. During this era and extending into the 1930s, these excursions crisscrossed the multi-colored deserts from Canyon de Chelly to the Grand Canyon and contributed significantly to the economy of the reservation.

Two traders of the period, Juan Lorenzo Hubbell of Ganado, Arizona, and John B. Moore of Crystal, new Mexico, greatly influenced the growth of the craft. Hubbell demanded quality, discouraging inferior dyes and loose-woven fabrics. He encouraged a return to Late

Hubbell's office showing wall hangings of commissioned art work of rug designs. *Photo courtesy of National Park Service.*

Hubbell Trading Post, 1890.
Obviously posed, this scene illustrates the prolific rug market which existed near the turn of the century. Hubbell (foreground) apparently chose to exhibit and publicize his inventory of Chief Blanket-type rugs, indicating its enduring popularity. He is seated upon a rather large example, facing no doubt its creator. Another Chief-designed fabric is "clotheslined" on the left, while three more can be identified hanging from the post walls in the background. Note the extremely large Ganado-style rug draped on the fence to the right; this size trait was a Hubbell specialty. The rug is now in a collection at the Museum of Northern Arizona in Flagstaff. *Photo courtesy of Museum of New Mexico.*

"Harveycar" and Indian Detour guests in New Mexico, circa 1929. *Courtesy of Museum of New Mexico.*

Rough Rock Trading Post, 1987.

Classic Period designs of bold crosses, stripes and diamonds, which were set against a brilliant red, aniline-dyed background that was bordered in black. He commissioned artists E. A. Burbank, Bertha A. Little and others to paint rug patterns in oil and watercolor, and these samples were hung in his post for weavers to copy. Hubbell also urged the weaving of heavier products — durable pieces in larger sizes to be used as area rugs in the home. In return, he promised "his" weavers higher sales in a greater market. The Fred Harvey Company stocked hundreds of the famed "Ganado reds" in their tourist outlets along the Santa Fe Railroad, and the rug became famous.[13]

John B. Moore was also a disciple of craftsmanship. He had weavers bring in raw wool which he then sent to eastern mills for machine cleaning.[14] When returned, the processed wool could be spun and woven more evenly. The technical quality of Moore-based rugs met with immediate success. Like Hubbell, he published mail-order catalogs outlining grades of wool, classes of rugs, and prices. These now out-of-print and rare booklets were illustrated with photographs of weavers at work and contained color plates of Navajo rugs. His distinctive styles included a bordered rug with the natural wool tones of black, brown and white, coupled with carded blends of gray, tan and beige and were used in combinations with commercial dyes of red and blue. Moore's greatest contribution was perhaps the designs that he originated. In later years, his basic patterns would give rise to another popular regional style rug called the *Two Grey Hills.*

Beginning in 1910, Navajo weaving started a descent into its second depression. During this time the federal government, hoping to increase meat production for the tribe, introduced large flocks of French Rambouillet sheep to the reservation. The new animal was a good producer, both in mutton and fleece, but for weaving purposes it was a disaster. The new wool was short and oily, difficult to clean, card, spin and weave. Many rugs coming off the loom were heavy and coarse textured. The white patterns showed dirty gray casts, and when dyed with bright colors, the wool reflected a loss of brilliance. Designs became stereotyped, causing prices and demand to fall drastically in some areas. To stimulate production, traders began buying rugs by weight (called "pound rugs"). Weavers soon responded to this and began to weave the wool without eliminating grease and dirt, thus increasing its weight. Some weavers went to such extremes as to saturate their rugs with "rubbed-in" dirt. Penalties were imposed for this practice, but it could not be controlled. By the late 1920s, a gloom of lost initiative had settled over some weaving areas on the reservation.

Extra fine and perfectly cleaned, per piece, $10.00 to $50.00 each, according to size and quality.

I have no saddle blankets nor common ones to quote.

Any of the grade will be shipped on approval with the understanding that the customer assumes all transportation costs both ways in case of return; and that no deductions on this account be allowed from invoice price in case of acceptance. We will ship, prepay, allow deductions from invoice price, on the extra fine ones of this grade, priced per piece, just the same as on the "ER-20" class, but only on these, of this "T-XX" class.

A FEW HINTS FOR THE CUSTOMER IN ORDERING

You always get the best value for your money in the higher priced rugs. You will be, and must be, pleased in these, and are assured against the possibility of buying and paying for a thing not satisfactory, by the return privilege allowed on all fine rugs.

You get just the size, the colors, and the pattern wanted, if you order from the "ER-20" class. If it is not in stock when your order comes, and you are willing to allow us a reasonable time in which to have it done, we will have it made for you especially. In this way you get something exclusive without the least danger of any other ever having something just like it.

Do not order the best quality and stipulate the lowest price. We wish in all cases to give the best possible value for the money and know that we do it, but I nor no other can sell our best goods for our lowest prices.

(Continued on page 25)

By permission Sim Schwemberger

NAVAJO RUG IN THE MAKING   The finished job
(Do you recognize the XXIV pattern?)

A sample page from the 1911 Moore catalog. John B. Moore is shown with one of "his" weavers illustrating a "top-of-the-line, ER-20 grade rug". Note the broad border, latch-hook elements and central cross patterns. All are characteristically Moore favorites, which may have been Mediterranean inspired. *Reproduced from* The Navajo, *1911. Courtesy of Gallup, New Mexico Public Library.*

Revival Period (1930-1940) — As is generally the case in most individual endeavors, a period of deterioration is usually followed by one of distinction. Some dedicated person or persons takes on the task for reversing the tide and thus brings forth a new level transcending all previous efforts.

Several persons were responsible for the craft's second rejuvenation. Most notable were Inja and Leon H. McSparron of Chinle, Arizona. By the early 1930s, in association with a Navajo benefactress named Mary C. Wheelwright, they undertook a program to encourage weavers of that district to experiment with the old vegetal-dye methods that were used prior to introduction of commercial colorants of the late 1870s. The Chinle weavers ultimately developed pastel hues of browns, golds and greens in Classic Period patterns of simple stripes and bands set on a borderless fabric — thus the *Chinle* regional style was conceived.

Encouraged by the restoration of soft vegetal-dye tones, but desiring a more varied color palate, Miss Wheelwright questioned the feasibility of creating such colors from commercial dyes. Subsequently, tests were initiated with the DuPont Chemical Company. The result was a series of manufactured dyes in a highly concentrated form, using 28 percent acetic acid as a mordant to be mixed with a desired colorant. In 1932, the dyes were introduced on the reservation. The solutions resulted in beautifully colored yarns, and weavers were pleased by the flexibility of tones that could be achieved. In the months that followed, the Diamond Dye Company of Burlington, Vermont, produced an improved series called *Old Navaho*. This product combined in one package the mordant with the colorant, thus relieving the weaver of the hazardous procedures of acid mixings. Today, the *Chinle* regional style rug reflects both the vegetal and commercial dye experiments of the Revival Period.

Further experimentation with native plant dyes was undertaken in the late 1930s by Bill and Sallie Lippincott of Wide Ruins Trading Post. They encouraged area weavers in the selection of subtle colors. Their labors met with excellent results, giving rise to a distinctive, well-woven product called the *Wide Ruins*, which today denotes an all-vegetal dyed rug.

The success of vegetal dyes did not end with the field tests at Chinle and Wide Ruins, but were carried on further in laboratory experiments at Fort Wingate Vocational High School east of Gallup, New Mexico. Here two women, Nonabah G. Bryan and Stella Young, conducted six years of research on native plants. A combination which resulted in 84 shades of color dyes. Findings of their study were published in 1940 under the title, *Navajo Native Dyes, Their Preparation and Use*, by the U.S. Department of the Interior. The recipe, instruction-type manual was widely circulated both on and off the reservation, and for those weavers who desired to work with vegetal-dye methods, the step-by-step procedures became

Commissioner Collier and unidentified Navajo elder, 1933. *Photo courtesy of National Park Service.*

an invaluable aid. In recent years, over 240 color tones have been achieved from native plant dyes, and the combinations from them are innumerable. This research and its applications represent one of the greatest contributions to Navajo weaving. The improved aesthetic quality of the vegetal-dye products, in the eyes of the white man, has in all probability extended the life of the craft.

Several other significant events occurred before the close of the Revival Period. First, overgrazing on range lands by rapidly increasing sheep flocks had first been identified as early as 1880. Government requested (voluntary) stock reductions had been unsuccessful and by 1920, a struggle began to emerge between what federal officials perceived to be prudent land management and what the Navajo culture held to be sacred gifts — their animals. In a 1933 decision, Commissioner John Collier implemented a hastily, poorly planned Stock Reduction Program which included law-enforced reductions of all flocks and herds on the reservation, regardless of size and ownership. To decree that all animals were to be lessened equally was terribly inequitable, as it had little effect on large operations, while small herders were virtually wiped out. Understandably, chaos developed out of the program with some areas actually experiencing wasteful slaughter of animals to meet mandatory numbers. The economic impact in wool, mutton, hide and rug losses was significant for a time, not to mention imposing poverty levels on some family units in declining livelihoods. Fortunately, the program was reevaluated and the reservation was divided into grazing districts requiring permits in relation to animal/pasturage ratios. The emotional pain of the Stock Reduction Program remains with the Navajo to this day, and is second only to the "Long Walk" in its trauma.

On a more positive note was the establishment of the Navajo Sheep Breeding Laboratory at Fort Wingate in 1934. Directed by the U.S. Department of Agriculture, programs were initiated to improve the Rambouillet strain, mainly through selective breeding with existing flocks. The success of the project provided a balance between high mutton yield and finer grades of fleece. Another plus was the founding of the Navajo Arts and Crafts Guild in 1941. This Window Rock-based organization provided quality controls and protection for the weaver, as well as assistance in procurement of good weaving materials and fair market outlets.

Regional Style Period (1940-Present) — As previously outlined, four areas were beginning to emerge as style centers in preceding periods — the Moore *Crystal* and Hubbell *Ganado* during the Rug Period (1890-1920), and the McSparron *Chinle* and Lippincott *Wide Ruins* in the Revival Period (1920-1940). Early in the development of the Regional Style Period, weavers in other areas sought to create new designs, ideas and arrangements of patterns and colors that would be commercially attractive. Those rugs whose history began with imaginative traders became the standard bearers of the period. Other areas at one time or another that were considered style centers, but failing to develop distinction through trader encouragement and guidance, or through merging of characteristics with stronger centers, soon lost their identities.

By the 1940s, the *Two Grey Hills* rug and the Shiprock *Yei* had also achieved regional style status. In the 1950s, there were five additional style-type rugs that were recognized and associated with certain geographic locations on the reservation: *Teec Nos Pos, Lukachukai,* the "new" *Crystal,* and the area designated as Western Reservation for the *Storm Pattern* style. Some writers recognize different separations in regional style weaving centers *(see correlation chart, p. 30-31)*. Each of these regional types is different, characterized by its own distinctive style, color, dye and design that can be identified at a glance as to its weaving center. In succeeding years an element of pride developed in these centers to emphasize the individualism of style.[15]

It is interesting to note that while the regional style rug is the most publicized textile in Navajoland at the present time, it accounts for only about 25 percent of total rug production. There is no law governing regional style weaving. Some weavers, regardless of their reservation home, may prefer the vegetal dyes and designs of a *Crystal* while residing near Ganado. A few are classed as combination weavers. These rare artists, who usually live in the vicinity of two rug regions, can produce two styles of design of equal excellence. Not all weavers are geared to regional styles. The majority like to combine styles, experiment with dyes, color arrangements and designs, and more or less create something entirely different from what is normally created in the region in which they live. The resulting pieces are called general rugs. Another type of weaver who does excellent work is the artist who undertakes to create a difficult specialty, such as the *Two-Faced, Pictorial, Sandpainting* and *Raised Outline* products. In the better quality weaves, these rugs often command higher prices than the regional pieces. Another often overlooked woven style is the *Saddle Blanket.* Hundreds of these less expensive, coarsely made, simply designed fabrics come off the reservation annually. Demand for these pieces remains fairly constant, not only because they are functional as horse trappings but they also serve as colorful, durable floor items.

The approximate breakdown of present rug production types on the reservation is as follows:

General Rugs......................................40%
Saddle Blankets..................................30%
Regional Style Rugs............................25%
Specialty Rugs....................................5%

Navajo rugs produced during the Regional Style Period represent the craft at its peak of artistic expression and acceptance. Versatility and quality are high, with some experts claiming finer craftsmanship, color balance and design than at any time in the history of the craft.

From the inception of the Regional Style Period the number of rugs gradually decreased. Prices began to soar in the early 1960s, with an annual increase at about 20 percent. Buyers were demanding quality, and only the talented weaver could realize the full worth of her product.

In the early 1970s, weaving was not economically attractive for the average weaver; many were not following in the avocation and others were becoming better educated and leaving the reservation for more lucrative employment. In 1973, in the Crystal and Lukachukai areas alone, there were only five name weavers remaining.

A spark of new life was regenerated in 1974 with the introduction and acceptance of the *Burntwater* regional style rug. However, by the 1980s, some writers, collectors (and even traders) were still predicting the demise of the craft before the beginning of the new century.

In the decade that has nearly passed, a resurgence has taken place that has production dramatically increased, artistic quality at an all-time high and prices soaring; the reason — commercial yarn and/or processed wool.[16]

The usage of these products in rug weaving are now entrenched in the craft, and it is estimated that 80 percent of all rugs coming off the Navajo loom today are constructed with either or both of these material types.

Commercial yarn relieves the weaver of the tedious tasks of wool preparation by 50 percent, thus increasing productivity and ensuring a greater profit margin (*see time/cost ratio chart, p.29*). Other advantages include the multiple range of yarn colors, including subtle pastel shades. This wide selection provides the expert weaver with an unlimited palate of diversity that allows their talent and creativity as an artist to expand in fashioning elaborately designed products of excellent quality.[17]

But all is not well with this approach. The "purist" regards rugs made with commercial yarn as non-traditional, while the "modernist" claims convenience and the production of a more evenly stitched and aesthetically pleasing fabric in half the time. Some dealers and serious collectors will not purchase rugs made of commercial yarn and feel that unsuspecting buyers should be made aware of what type of materials are being used. Judges at some weaving competitions argue that authenticity requires that a "true" Navajo rug be totally handmade. This includes the wool, which has to be sheared, cleaned, hand carded, handspun and dyed in a traditional manner. In some shows, where two rugs of equal quality in artistic expression and construction are being considered, preference will be given to the weaver who has prepared the wool.

Commercial yarn and/or processed wool is not new to the reservation. During the Late Classic Period, bayeta and flannel threads were used in combinations with Saxony yarns, followed by Germantown yarns in the Transition Period. John B. Moore was the first to see the benefits in reducing the steps of rug making. He arranged for processed wool to be utilized in the rugs that he sold, and advertised the fact that he was using processed wool in his 1911 catalog. No objections were raised during these periods, nor in the intervening years when some commercial yarn and processed wool were undoubtedly available at the counters in most trading posts. The prevalence in modern times, however, of almost total use of commercial yarn is what some critics are predicting will be disastrous; that is, a complete loss of traditional wool preparation skills. This may be the strongest argument, for if the trend continues, a "real" Navajo rug that is procured from the back of a sheep, that is hand cleaned, hand carded, handspun, hand dyed and ultimately woven, will indeed be a rare item.

Change is inevitable, and the Navajo is adaptable. The reservation is now experiencing greater mobility, increased awareness and with the old trading post system being replaced by tribal-operated convenience stores, many aspects of the Navajo culture are becoming "Anglicized".

The Regional Style Period is coming to a close. Most of the rug style names will probably continue, but the geographic boundaries that spawned the period are now fused. What used to be identifiable patterns, designs and dyes associated with a specific locale are obsolete, as weavers are becoming more versatile in their creations. Except in a few cases, the influence of the area trader in weaving is also gone, and no longer does the expert weaver have to depend on the trading post as a marketing center. They now express their individuality and, if necessary, will travel hundreds of miles to places like Albuquerque and Scottsdale to get the best price. Arts and crafts dealers (and collectors) are in constant ploys with each other to gain the favored textiles from the name weavers, thus again bypassing the trading post.[18] Commissioned rugs have come into play, with recognized weavers offering their work even before the loom is warped. In short, quality sells and production is hard pressed to keep up with demand — at any price.

So, as the craft progresses into the 21st century, what is next? Some predict acrylic yarns/nylon warp, mechanical looms and mass production. Others are hopeful that some intangible force will intercede, and a rebirth into a "traditional period" might begin. What may prevail, from all indications, is an entry into a precarious "commercial period".

In any event, for whatever the future holds, history will always deal kindly with the spirited resolve of the craft. In its 300-year plight, it has survived three economic depressions, imprisonment of its makers, partial relocation and what with borrowed ingredients like the Pueblo loom, Spanish and French sheep, German and English yarn, Mexican designs and American dyes, it has managed amazingly well in spite of it all. The rug came into being because the white man accepted a textile that satisfied his aesthetic needs at a particular time, and because of it, the white man has come to a better understanding of the red man.

Weavers at the loom, 1890. *Courtesy of National Park Service.*

Chapter 2

FROM SHEEP TO RUG

Navajo weaver and friend.

The Sheep

The Navajo people lead a pastoral existence. They are "sheep-minded"; from sunup to sundown their main concern is for their flocks. The herding life is strenuous, especially in winter months when snow blankets the sparse grasslands, forcing herds into constant wandering in search of food.

The "Navajo sheep" is not a particular breed. The principal flocks raised on the reservation are a mixture of various strains, including the French Rambouillet blood lines of the Merino breed supplemented with Corriedale rams. The dominant ancestry is still probably the old Spanish churro. The fleece is relatively heavy, yielding approximately 8-10 pounds per animal.

Shearing

The first step in conversion of wool to rug is shearing, usually accomplished in early spring when the fleece has attained its greatest thickness. Small portions of the flock are corralled at a time, whereupon the shearer will sweep a sand-cleared spot on the ground and commence with the flanking and ultimate trimming of the animal; ordinarily metal shears are used. There is no system to the operation, although a skillful worker will clip from the neck toward the tail, making efforts to keep the fleece in one piece. The select wool is obtained from the back, at the shoulders and along the flanks. The remaining shorter fibers are separated and bagged for sale at the trading post.

Cleaning

Shorn wool, earmarked for weaving, is then hand cleaned of burrs, sticks and other debris. A fluffing technique accompanies the general cleaning, and the wool is laid out for a short period for airing and drying of animal oils. Some weavers sprinkle white clay or pulverized selenite (gypsum) on the fleece to absorb oil and dirt. If the shorn wool is exceptionally dirty, a wet washing may then be necessary to remove saturated impurities.

Carding

The purpose of carding is to straighten the tangled fibers into loose, uniform pads. Small handfuls of the washed wool are hand fluffed and then raked across two hand-held, metal-toothed towcards. This technique combs the wool into slender fibers that can be easily spun. Carding also serves as a second cleaning. Persistent friction of the forward and backward towing removes most remaining particles of grit. Carding is the least enjoyable task in the rug process. It requires considerable strength in the hands and arms in an unnatural cramped position. Recently, more weavers are turning to commercial and/or processed wool, which can be purchased at off-reservation outlets.

Spinning

This process determines the strength and weight of the rug. The Navajo technique of spinning remains as traditional as the craft itself. No machine procedure is involved. Instead, a simple spindle stick and whorl, about 12" long, resembling a miniature ski pole, is manipulated with the hands. The base of the spindle is seated on the ground with the shaft twirled on the thigh with one hand, while the other hand regulates thickness of the fiber. Two spinnings are usually required to produce weft yarns. Additional respinnings will produce finer and finer threads, thus resulting in a more finely woven rug. If a weaver chooses, they can bypass the spinning step and purchase commercial pre-spun yarn, usually in a wide range of colors, over the counter.

Washing

Before the yarn is dyed, it is necessary that it be washed. The only soap the early weavers knew, and which is still preferred by many, was the high lathers obtained from roots of the broad-leaved Yucca, mainly Yucca *baccata* that is obtained in central parts of the reservation and the narrow-leafed Yuccas, such as *glauca* and Yucca *standleyi*. Both agents can be used fresh or dried and may be gathered at any season of the year. The broad-leaved Yucca is the stronger and more desirable of the two. After a thorough washing, including at least two rinses, care is taken not to squeeze, twist, or "wring out" the wool, as it promotes lumping and knotting of the fibers. Instead, the wool should be floated freely in the water and removed carefully and placed on boards and rocks for sun drying.

Dyeing

Various degrees of color can be achieved by the modern weaver. In some cases a combination will prevail in a single rug. In the natural wool tones, such as a *Two Grey Hills*, shades of tan, beige and gray can be attained in the carding step by blending desired amounts of black, brown and white wools.[19] In other instances, bright commercial synthetic dyes, purchased over the counter, can be used in addition to vegetal-dyed wools. If a weaver wishes to dye the yarn, it is done after the spinning and washing.

Vegetal-dyed techniques require considerable more time and effort for preparation of the yarn. Bryan and Young (1940, p. 9) outline the following procedures for the dyeing of one color:

> She selects an enamel kettle for dyeing, because she found that if she does it in tin or aluminum the acid developed in the dyebath while fermenting reacts upon the metal, and the color of the dye is changed. She measures

out the dried prickly pear fruit and covers it with lukewarm water to soak overnight. In the morning she mashes it well, strains it, and adds enough more cool water to cover the yarn completely. She then places the wet yarn in it, rubs the dye into it well, covers it, and sets it in a warm place for ferment, having learned from previous experience that if she boils it the lovely rose color will change to tan. Many times each day during the following weeks she rubs the dye into the yarn. If she finds at the end of the time that the rose color is not as deep as she wishes it, she puts it in another dyebath of the same strength as before and allows it to ferment another week. She then rinses it thoroughly and hangs it up to dry.

Bryan and Young (1940) follow with a list of ten basic observations that should be heeded in the vegetal dyeing of wool:

Display of partial vegetal-dye colors and sources.

1) The same species of plant grown in different sections of the country may give different shades of color. The shade of color may also vary from year to year from a plant grown in the same locality.

2) All dye plants may be used with or without a mordant. The use of a mordant deepens the color and occasionally changes it. The use of a different mordant, or varying the quantity of mordant used, also produces a difference in the color given by the same plant. Colors dyed without a mordant are reasonably fast.

3) Longer boiling of the dye with the yarn usually produces a deeper color. Occasionally the color is entirely changed.

4) Allowing the yarn to remain in the dyebath overnight deepens and brightens the color. It is believed that it also produces a faster color.

5) It is necessary that most of the dyes be boiled with the yarn to produce the color. There are exceptions to this, however. Cactus fruit, some berries and flowers lose their color when boiled. For this reason we allow the dye to ferment into the yarn as explained in the recipes.

6) The afterbath yarn, or the second yarn dyed in the same dyewater, is a softer, lighter tint of the same color.

7) Most of the plants may be used either fresh or dried. Fresh plants are usually stronger than when dried. Therefore, less of the fresh is required to produce the same color. Dried canaigre root, however, is stronger than when it is fresh. One must bear this in mind when substituting in the following recipes.

8) Dried barks, plants, and fruits should be soaked overnight before using.

9) Yarns must be rinsed several times after dyeing to remove the unabsorbed dye.

10) The yarns dyed by the following recipes have been tested for color fastness when treated with commercial cleaners and moth preventives and were found to be unchanged by them.

In arriving at colors in vegetal dyeing, the yellows are the easiest to obtain, and range from bright yellow through greenish yellow to mustard to gold. The browns have a range from beige to dark-colored browns to deep rose and rich tans. The most frequently found colors are orange, gray, tan, coral, brown, yellow and variable tints of rose. A deep red is the hardest to obtain, as is a good solid green, both usually requiring additional color baths. Listed below are the 84 basic sources and colors found in Bryan and Young (1940). This is by no means the complete color range of vegetal dyes. The shades, tints, hues and combinations of plant colors reach infinity. The following examples form the basis of plant usage now generally in practice on the reservation. In several instances, one plant can produce several hues of color. This can be accomplished by controlling the strength of the dyebath (cooking time) and varying the recipe (amount of vegetal matter used).

Partial List of Vegetal-Dye Colors and Sources

No.	Colors	Source
1	Light greenish-yellow	Actinea flower, multiple flower (flowers and leaves)
2	Yellow	Actinea flower, single-flowered (flowers and leaves)
3	Soft brown	Alder tree (bark)
4	Tan-beige	Alder tree (bark)
5	Yellow-green	Beeplant (leaves)
6	Greenish-yellow	Bitterball (leaves)
7	Pale greenish-yellow	Bitterball (leaves)
8	Mustard	Bitterball (leaves)
9	Rose	Prickly Pear Cactus
10	Deep rose	Prickly Pear Cactus
11	Light rose	Prickly Pear Cactus
12	Pink with a light tan	Prickly Pear Cactus
13	Tan	Prickly Pear cactus
14	Coral pink	Prickly Pear cactus and Mountain Mahogany (root bark)
15	Medium brown	Canaigre (roots)
16	Yellow-orange	Canaigre (roots)
17	Light canary-yellow	Wild celery (flowers)
18	Bright yellow	Chamizo (leaves, twigs and blossoms)
19	Light canary-yellow	Chamizo (leaves, twigs and blossoms)
20	Mustard	Chamizo (leaves, twigs and blossoms)
21	Purplish-brown	Chokeberry (root bark) and Wild plum (root bark)
22	Bright yellow	Owls' claws (leaves, twigs and blossoms)
23	Light canary-yellow	Owls' claws (leaves, twigs and blossoms)
24	Mustard	Owls' claws (leaves, twigs and blossoms)
25	Dulled greenish-yellow	Oregon Grape (roots, leaves and stems)
26	Light gray	Ironwood (berries)
27	Orange tan	One-seeded juniper (twigs)
28	Yellow tan	One-seeded juniper (twigs)
29	Greenish-gray	Wild Purple Larkspur (petals)
30	Light greenish-yellow	Wild Purple Larkspur (flowers, leaves and stems)
31	Light orange	Ground lichen
32	Reddish-tan	Ground lichen
33	Yellow-tan	Ground lichen
34	Greenish-yellow	Blue-flowered Lupine (flowers, leaves and stems)
35	Soft reddish-brown	Mountain Mahogany (root bark)
36	Deep reddish-brown	Mountain Mahogany (root bark) with Juniper ashes
37	Rose taupe	Mountain Mahogany (root bark) with Cactus fruit
38	Soft reddish-tan	Mountain Mahogany (root bark) with Cactus fruit
39	Dark burnt-orange	Mountain Mahogany (root bark) with Navajo tea
40	Henna	Mountain Mahogany (root bark) with Navajo tea
41	Light red-brown	Mountain Mahogany (root bark) with ground lichens
42	Light brown	Mountain Mahogany (root bark) with Alder bark
43	Reddish-tan	Mountain Mahogany (root bark) with Alder bark
44	Soft cream-tan	Mountain Mahogany (root bark) with Alder bark
45	Light brown	Mountain Mahogany (root bark) with Alder bark

46	Dulled tan	Gambel Oak (bark)
47	Light gold	Scrub Oak (gall)
48	Light yellowish-tan	Scrub Oak (gall)
49	Tan	Indian Paintbrush (blossoms)
50	Greenish-yellow	Indian Paintbrush (leaves, stems and blossoms)
51	Dull tan	Pinedrop (entire plant)
52	Reddish-purple	Wild plum (roots)
53	Bright yellow	Rabbitbrush, large (blossoms and twigs)
54	Light canary-yellow	Rabbitbrush, large (blossoms and twigs)
55	Mustard	Rabbitbrush, large (blossoms and twigs)
56	Bright yellow	Rabbitbrush, small (blossoms and twigs)
57	Light canary-yellow	Rabbitbrush, small (blossoms and twigs)
58	Mustard	Rabbitbrush, small (blossoms and twigs)
59	Gold	Cliff rose (twigs and leaves)
60	Bright yellow	Rubberplant (leaves, stems and flowers)
61	Light canary-yellow	Rubberplant (leaves, stems and flowers)
62	Mustard	Rubberplant (leaves, stems and flowers)
63	Slight greenish-yellow	Basin sagebrush (leaves and twigs)
64	Pale greenish-yellow	Basin sagebrush (leaves and twigs)
65	Mustard	Basin sagebrush (leaves and twigs)

66	Gold	Basin sagebrush (leaves and twigs)
67	Rich olive-green	Basin sagebrush (leaves and twigs)
68	Medium olive-green	Basin sagebrush (leaves and twigs)
69	Bluish black	Sumac (leaves), Piñon pitch, yellow ocher
70	Light oxford-gray	Sumac (leaves), Piñon pitch, yellow ocher
71	Light orange-brown	Sumac (berries)
72	Light tan	Mormon tea (twigs and leaves)
73	Orange	Navajo tea (flowers)
74	Light orange	Navajo tea (flowers)
75	Light olive-green	Navajo tea (leaves)
76	Orange	Navajo tea (leaves and flowers) and Canaigre (root)
77	Pine needle green	Navajo tea (leaves) and black dyewater
78	Dull olive-green	Russian thistle (entire plant)
79	Deep tan	Russian thistle (young plant)
80	Rich brown	Wild walnut hulls
81	Gray tan	Wild walnut hulls
82	Rich tan	Wild walnut hulls
83	Light tan	Wild walnut (leaves)
84	Salmon pink	Brick-colored rainwater from red mesas in Arizona and New Mexico

Legend of Spider Woman

Spider Woman instructed the Navajo women how to weave on a loom which Spider Man told them how to make. The crosspoles were made of sky and earth cords, the warp sticks of sun rays, the heddles of rock crystal and sheet lightning. The batten was a sun halo, white shell made the comb. There were four spindles: one stick of zigzag lightning with a whorl of cannel coal, one a stick of flash lightning with a whorl of turquoise, a third had a stick of sheet lightning with a whorl of abalone, a rain streamer formed the stick of the fourth, and its whorl was white shell.

Crosspiece
Upright
Stick

Warp beam

Warp threads

Shed rod

Heddle rod

Web beam

Cross piece

The Loom

The Navajo loom consists of two uprights and two crosspieces of log-size wood 6" to 8" in diameter, usually cut from small pine trees. The lower crosspiece, serving as the base, must be composed of the heaviest wood to support the balance of the frame. Legs of wood may be constructed at right angles to the uprights to serve as additional support. It is very important that the entire structure be rigid.

Warping The Loom

When the weaver has determined the size of the rug that is to be woven, the warp thread is prepared.[20] The warp thread, or strand, serves as the foundation of the rug. It is necessarily stronger to support the total body of woven wefts. The stringing of the warp is done on a warpframe, a temporary device separated from the loom proper, consisting of two long boards forming the sides and two securely tied crosspieces (usually of 1" dowel or broomstick size) at each end. The warpframe is laid horizontally on the ground, elevated a few inches by rocks at the four corners. If there is sufficient room inside the warpframe (considering the size of the proposed rug), the weaver can be positioned within the enclosure to begin with the stringing.

The warp is one continuous strand that is wound in a figure-eight pattern at approximately 1/4-inch intervals around the two dowel crosspieces. Constant tension of the warp is maintained as the strand is passed over the dowel on the outside and returned under the dowel on the inside, thus creating warp pairs. The two figure eight patterns created are called sheds, established by the insertion and tying of two sticks, called shed rods, into the warp pattern. During actual weaving, manipulation of the shed rods creates the needed spaces for passing of the weft threads. To secure their equally spaced position on the dowel, the warp is then edged off by a twining cord to form a stabilizing top and bottom border.

When the entire warp is strung and secured, the warpframe is dismantled and the warp is transferred and mounted on the permanent upright loom by lashing the warp dowels, now referred to as the warp beam (upper) and the web beam (lower), with a lightweight rope. The warp beam is actually attached to another dowel, called the stick, that can be rope-lowered or raised to desired heights. The shed rods are then untied but not removed. The warp is straightened within the loom frame and a desired tension is applied to make the entire harness a taut unit.

Weaving

The basic Navajo weave is the tapestry technique in which the warp threads are completely concealed by passage of the weft yarn.[21] To facilitate passing of the wefts through the warp lines, the shed rods are employed. The upper shed rod is a loosely inserted stick placed between alternating warps. The lower shed rod (sometimes called a heddle rod) is secured to opposite alternating warp threads. By manipulating shed rod and heddle, odd numbered warps can be brought forward and separated from even- numbered warps. To enlarge the opening for weaving, a flat stick called a batten (18" to 24" long, 1" wide) is inserted and turned on edge. The wefts ultimately are tamped into place by a wooden-toothed comb called the fork.

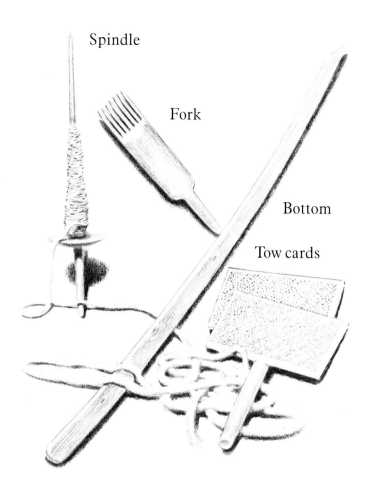

The designs that originate in a rug generally evolve in the imagination of the weaver before the actual weaving takes place. Traditional Navajo designs usually are handed down from one generation to another. As a result, a repetition of colors and basic motifs can prevail in a weaving family.

According to Bill Malone, trader at Hubbell Trading Post, a good to average weaver can accomplish approximately one square foot of weave per day.[22]

When the rug is completed, the weaver offers the finished product for sale at the trading post. Recognizing the value and time that was spent on the rug, they will understandably negotiate for the best price possible. If necessary, they will try several neighboring posts (or off-reservation outlets) until satisfaction is met. During earlier times when travel was somewhat restricted on the reservation, rugs were sold in proximity to the weaver's home. Today, with the ubiquitous pickup truck speeding along on improved highways, weavers may travel hundreds of miles to get their asking price. Considering this "roaming about" of rugs, it may be confusing at times to see a particular regional style, such as a *Crystal*, on the rack at Hubbell Trading Post, or a *Ganado* at Teec Nos Pos.[23] For this reason then, many reservation outlets now stock a good selection of representative rug styles. If a purchaser is not aware of identifying characteristics, it is easy to be misled. One of the most common mistakes made in regional style names is to label a rug by the trading post from which it was purchased.

Correlation Chart of Regional

James, 1999 (this publication)	Rodee, 1987	Tanner, 1968
1. Shiprock	1. Four Corners 2. Red Rock	1. Farmington—Shiprock
2. Lukachukai (?)	----------------------------------	2. Lukachukai—Greasewood
3. Teec Nos Pos	3. Teec Nos Pos 4. Red Mesa	3. Teec Nos Pos
4. Crystal	5. Crystal	4. Crystal
5. Two Grey Hills	6. Two Grey Hills	5. Two Grey Hills
6. Chinle (?)	7. Chinle 8. Nazlini	6. Chinle
7. Ganado	9. Ganado	7. Ganado 8. Kayenta
8. Wide Ruins	10. Wide Ruins 11. Pine Springs	9. Wide Ruins 10. Pine Springs
9. Western Reservation (?)	----------------------------------	11. Western Reservation
10. Burntwater	12. Burntwater	----------------------------------
11. New Lands (?)	----------------------------------	----------------------------------
----------------------------------	----------------------------------	12. Gallup
----------------------------------	----------------------------------	13. Coal Mine Mesa
----------------------------------	----------------------------------	----------------------------------

(?) Questionable at this time as to status as a regional style (*see Additional Note 15*).

Style Weaving Centers

Bahti, 1966	Maxwell, 1963	Kent, 1961
1. Shiprock—Lukachukai	1. Shiprock	1. Shiprock
--------------------------------	2. Lukachukai	2. Lukachukai
2. Teec Nos Pos	3. Teec Nos Pos 4. Red Mesa	3. Teec Nos Pos
3. Crystal	5. Crystal	4. Crystal
4. Two Grey Hills	6. Two Gray Hills	5. Two Gray Hills
5. Chinle 6. Nazlini	7. Chinle	6. Chinle
7. Ganado 8. Klagetoh	8. Ganado 9. Keams Canyon—Piñon	7. Ganado 8. Keams Canyon
9. Wide Ruins	10. Wide Ruins	9. Wide Ruins
10. Western Reservation	11. Western Reservation	10. Western Reservation
--------------------------------	--------------------------------	--------------------------------
--------------------------------	--------------------------------	--------------------------------
11. Gallup	12. Gallup	11. Coal Mine Mesa
12. Coal Mine Mesa	13. Coal Mine Mesa	12. Coppermine
--------------------------------	--------------------------------	13. Shonto— Navajo Mountain

Chapter 3

SHIPROCK
'A Place of Deity'

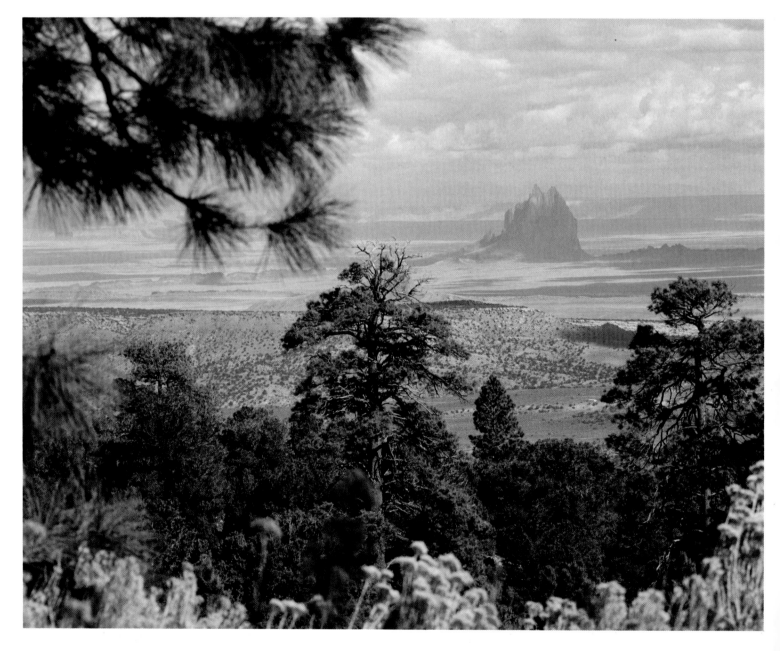

Shiprock — View is east from the Lukachukai Mountains.

The Post

The town of Shiprock (called Needles before 1848) is located on the San Juan River in extreme northwestern New Mexico. Its present name is derived from a volcanic neck called Shiprock, a towering igneous mass that dominates the landscape ten miles southwest of town. In Navajo mythology the majestic rock is called *Tse Bit'a'i*, meaning "Rock with Wings," or "Winged Rock".

In 1872, the Shiprock site was scouted by Thomas Keam for the federal government in an effort to establish a Fort Defiance sub-agency office. Plans for construction of the facility did not materialize until September 11, 1903. The first buildings were built of logs and adobe, later replaced by brick structures after the flood of 1911.

The first superintendent of the Shiprock Agency was W.T. Shelton, a man whose contribution to Navajo weaving has been largely overlooked in contemporary writings. In 1909, Shelton conceived the idea of holding Navajo fairs, inviting not only Indians, but traders as well, to display their extensive exhibits of Navajo craftsmanship. The Shiprock conclaves, held annually the first week of October, were a great success. The principal theme was the presentation of rugs and silversmithing for which

Rug displays at Shiprock Fair, 1912. These rare and informative photographs illustrate several important facts.
Top: Newly, brick-constructed Shiprock Agency buildings backdrop the fair displays. Chimney smoke and smoldering bonfire ashes (both photos) suggest a brisk early fall day. Unexplained erroneous spelling of H.B. Noel's Teec Nos Pos sign ("East— Nos Pos") on the right. Note swastika designs in rug in the center: a John B. Moore favorite.
Bottom: The examples on the right, under the faintly visible Two Grey Hills banner, exhibit typical Crystal characteristics, which emphasize Moore's contribution in the development of the early Two Grey Hills rug. The modern-day Two Grey Hills did not emerge until the mid-1920s. Note the Storm Pattern elements in the third rug hanging from the right, another motif possibly attributed to Moore. The Yeis had not yet made their appearance by 1912. Most of the displayed examples reflect Teec Nos Pos outline designs. *Photos courtesy of Gilbert Maxwell & Best-West Publications.*

prizes were awarded. At the 1912 fair, over 400 pieces of weaving were displayed. The Navajos received valuable publicity from these fairs.

The first trading post in the area was operated as Robert Baker's Shiprock Trading Post. Bruce Bernard bought the Baker property in 1909 and operated it until his death in 1952. Another post, managed by theWalker and Hubbard Company, was purchased in 1912 by Will Evans. The Evans store was acquired by the Jacks brothers in the summer of 1948, who in turn sold out to Russell Foutz in 1954. The holdings were transferred in late 1972 to a nephew, Ed Foutz, who operates the post today as the Shiprock Trading Company.

The Rug

The Shiprock rug type is called a *Yei* (pronounced "yea"). It was developed by Will Evans around the World War I period from stylized sandpaintings. The *Yei* is a colorful piece that depicts religious figures (a deity), but has no religious significance. The rug is often of small to moderate size, carrying bright-colored, slender, front-facing figures surrounded by, in most cases, a multi-colored rainbow goddess that serves as a border down the sides and across the bottom. Additional designs may include interspacings of cornstalks and arrows. Backgrounds are usually white or light tan, with lesser amounts of dark and light blends of natural, handspun gray. The rug is finely woven with a growing use of commercial yarn. The *Yei* usually lends itself as a wall hanging in the same manner as a fine painting.

Another type of rug woven in the Shiprock area is the *Yeibechai*. Similar to the *Yei* in size, bright colors and commercial yarn, the *Yeibechai* is a bordered rug (sometimes incorporating a design) that illustrates Navajo dancers, usually in profile, impersonating *Yei* figures.[24]

Top right:
Plate 1
Shiprock Yei (27" X 41")
Weaver: Bernia Pettygras, Shiprock, NM
Source: Author's collection (1968)
Construction: Mostly synthetic dyed, some minor commercial yarn in outlines, processed white, natural carded gray, mostly handspun.

Center right:
Plate 2
Shiprock Yei (40" X 40")
Weaver: Unknown
Source: Courtesy of Covered Wagon, Albuquerque, NM (1970)
Construction: Synthetic-dyed figures and designs, processed white background, minor commercial yarn, mostly handspun.

Left:
Plate 3
Shiprock Yeibechai (30" X 36")
Weaver: Rose Peshlakai, Shiprock, NM
Source: Private collection (1970)
Construction:Synthetic dyed, processed white, all handspun.

Shiprock Area Map

20-Year Comparative Costs				Weavers
Year **3' x 5'**	**4' x 6'**	**6' x 9'**	**Large Specials**	Daisy Barton
1978 $200-500	$600-800	—		Lucy Farley
1988 $800-1,200	$1,500-3,000	—	$5,000+	Mary Long (combination Yei,
1998 $1,500-2,000	$3,000-5,000	$6,000-8,000	—	Teec Nos Pos, and Sandpainting weaver)
				Marie Peshlakai
				Lilly Touchin
Trading Posts		**Traders**		Lola Yazzie (combination Yei and
				Teec Nos Pos weaver)
Cove Trading Post		Raymond Ismay		
Red Rock Trading Post		Troy Kennedy		
Shiprock Trading Company		Ed Foutz		
Foutz Trading Company		Bill Foutz		

Chapter 4

LUKACHUKAI

'A Summer Place'

The Post

Lukachukai is pronounced "look-a-choo-ki" and translates from the Navajo meaning "white patch of reeds extends out". The settlement is located along the west base of an impressive red-rock escarpment of the Lukachukai Mountains. The immediate area is one of the most scenic on the reservation. Transition from a sage-covered plain to forests and meadows is quite abrupt, leading some writers to refer to the highlands as the "Navajo Alps". The Indians call the mountains *Shiink'eh*, or "Summer Place".

The first trading post was established in 1892 by George N. Barker. George Washington Sampson, a veteran trader who managed a chain of trading posts, operated the store for a time following the turn of the century. Some references include the name Rico Menapasé as being an active trader in the area, but no firm dates have been found to support his activities; possibly he occupied a brief time period between Sampson and W.R.Cassidy. A license transfer shows that Cassidy sold out to Earl Kennedy in October 1928. Earl's son, Kenneth, assumed managership of the store following his father's death in September 1971, and operated the post until its closure in 1979; the facility was later razed. The site, with only foundations remaining, is situated just north of Navajo Route 13 (1 mile east of the junction with Navajo Route 12) on a level shelf of land overlooking Lukachukai Creek. The lone remaining store at Lukachukai is located a short distance to the east where Bradley and Victoria Blair operate Totsoh Trading Post.

The Rug

The Lukachukai area is a second source of the *Yei* rug. Here, however, the figures are more massive in their presentation. In recent years, there has been a tendency towards the use of pastel-colored yarns to give the product a vegetal-dyed appearance. Backgrounds are usually grays, mustards, golds or brown colored. In most examples the rug has a border enclosing the rainbow goddess, usually in a bright color. In many pieces, the rainbow goddess is completely eliminated, with a solitary heavy border enclosing the figures. More figures occupy the *Lukachukai Yei*, but are less detailed and colorful. Also, the *Yei* figures tend to take on a more human appearance, similar to the frontal-facing *Yeibechais*. The basic motif is the same as in the rugs along the San Juan River, but as those to the northeast are suitable for the wall, the heavier, coarse-textured *Yeis* from across the intervening mountains are more adaptable as a floor covering.

Plate 4
Lukachukai Yei (36" X 60")
Weaver: Unknown
Source: Courtesy of Hubbell Trading Post, Ganado, AZ (1968)
Construction: Partly synthetic dyed, natural white, natural carded gray, some vegetal dyes, all handspun.

Plate 5
Lukachukai Yei (40" X 40")
Weaver: Unknown
Source: Courtesy of Hubbell Trading Post, Ganado, AZ (1968)
Construction: Partly synthetic dyed, natural white, some vegetal dyes, all handspun.

The Road to Lukachukai, 1973.

Lukachukai Area Map

Comparative Costs					Weavers
Year	3' x 5'	4' x 6'	6' x 9'	Large Specials	Nora Allen
					Mary Bahe
1978	$75-250	$300-500	$600-$1,200	—	Grace Bern
1988	$100-$250	$300-$500	$600-$1,200	—	Lucy Betony
1998	$250-500	$400-750	—	—	Rita Bitani
					Annie Brady
					Ella Gene
					Irma Higdon
Trading Posts		**Traders**			Annabelle Weaver
					Lois E. Wheeler
Round Rock Trading Post		C.E. Wheeler			
Totsoh Trading Post					
(Lukachukai)		Bradley and Victoria Blair			

Chapter 5

TEEC NOS POS
'Gateway to the Four Corners'

The Post

H.B. (Hambleton Bridger) Noel from Essex County, Virginia, was not a timid soul. He established his Teec Nos Pos Trading Post in 1905 in the remote area west of Shiprock, with full knowledge that predecessors had been chased out by local Indians. He bought a high-powered Remington rifle, and after impressing the Navajos with his prowess on how to use it, he hung the gun conspicuously on the wall back of the counter, in easy reach.

Teec Nos Pos Trading Post, 1973.

The improbable location that Noel chose was in foothills of the northern Carrizos, at the head of a cottonwood-lined canyon on Tisnosbas Creek. Furthermore, the bravery of the man led him into a region controlled by Black Horse, a Navajo headsman whose unruliness had inhibited trading ventures.[25] Before a single spade of dirt was turned, several hundred Navajos gathered at the canyon site to debate whether they should let this man with the corn-colored hair live among them. After a day-long council, the Indians voted to let him stay, because they respected his courage and it seemed that the time was right to link themselves to outside goods.

Noel traded at Teec Nos Pos for eight years, selling out to a partnership of Bert Dustin and Al Foutz and retiring to a farm along the San Juan River. Russell Foutz, of Fruitland, New Mexico, purchased the store in 1945. The old post was destroyed by fire in 1959 and was rebuilt the same year on a higher shelf of land a few miles to the north of its original location. Today, Teec Nos Pos has achieved a community atmosphere and is a busy trading crossroads, mainly because its strategic location serves as a gateway to the Four Corners Monument. Unfortunately, the place name, meaning "circle of cottonwoods," which described the original canyon setting, does not characterize the post's present location.

Noel's original Teec Nos Pos Trading Post, 1949. *Courtesy of Museum of New Mexico.*

The Rug

The dedicated weavers of Teec Nos Pos produce a tightly woven rug that has been described by many as the "least Navajo" of all the regional styles. The rug has a Persian flair, possibly influenced in part by John B. Moore of Crystal (*see* Chapter 6). Trader Noel took no credit for the design, and according to Maxwell (1963), credited a Mrs. Wilson, an area missionary, for directing the weavers in this style.

The *Teec Nos Pos* rug is very busy and intricate in design. Colors, often used in small jewel-like amounts, are rather flamboyant: bright greens, blues, oranges, and reds are popular. Commercial yarns are more often used, with some utilization of synthetic-dyed, handspun fibers. The typical *Teec Nos Pos* possesses a broad border that contains a design, usually in large H, T, or L arrangements. The rug primarily features a contrasting color outline of the main patterns which usually consist of zigzags, serrated diamonds, triangles and boxes. Because of its usually bright, multiple colors, the *Teec Nos Pos* is more difficult to blend into home decorating schemes.

Fifteen miles west of Teec Nos Pos lies the trading area of Red Mesa. Here, a small group of weavers are producing serrated, diamond-styled outline rugs that are reminiscent of the old "eyedazzlers". Usually designed with broad *Teec Nos Pos* borders, the wool usage is primarily traditional handspun yarns of grays, white, black, maroons and dark red. Some writers, because of the outline feature, have recognized the Red Mesa rug as a distinct regional style.

Plate 6
Teec Nos Pos (72" X 108")
Weaver: Unknown
Source: Courtesy of Covered Wagon, Albuquerque, NM (1970)
Construction: Synthetic dyed, processed white, all handspun.

Beautiful Mountain.

Plate 7
Teec Nos Pos (31" X 44")
Weaver: Unknown
Source: Courtesy of Covered Wagon, Albuquerque, NM (1970)
Construction: Synthetic dyed, processed white, all handspun.

Plate 8
Teec Nos Pos (48" X 72")
Weaver: Louise Cattleman, Teec Nos Pos, AZ
Source: Private collection (1969)
Construction: Partly synthetic dyed, partly vegetal dyed, natural white, some minor commercial yarn, mostly handspun.

Teec Nos Pos Area Map

20-Year Comparative Costs				Weavers	
Year	**3' x 5'**	**4' x 6'**	**6' x 9'**	Dorothy Begay	Lilly Joan
			Large Specials	Hilda Begay	Mary C. Joe
				Nellie T. Begay	Alice Nelson
1978	$500-800	$800-1,200	$1,500-2,000 $2,500+	Louise Cattleman	
1988	$600-1,000	$1,500-1,800	$2,000-5,000 $6,000+	Mary Clark	
1998	$2,500-4,000	$4,000-7,500	$7,500-12,000 $15,000+	Connie Yabenay	
				Emma Yabenay	
Trading Posts		**Traders**		Ruth Yabenay	
				Marie Wallace	
Beclabito Trading Post		Jay and Lloyd Foutz		Mary White	
Sweetwater Trading Post		Wilbert Martin		Lola Yazzie	
Teec Nos Pos Trading Post		Larry Comer		Mary Long	

Chapter 6

CRYSTAL
'Where Crystal Water Flows Out'

Crystal Trading Post, 1973.

The Post

On September 3, 1849, Lieutenant James H. Simpson, diarist for the Navajo Reconnaissance Expedition under Colonel John M. Washington, included in his entry for the day:

> . . . I noticed towering pines and firs, also the oak, the aspen, and the willow; and bordering the stream was a great variety of shrubbery, the hop vine, loaded with its fruit, being intertwined among them. Flowers of rich profusion, and of every hue and delicacy, were also constantly before the eye — upwards of ninety varieties having been picked up since we entered the gorge [Washington Pass] yesterday. Indeed we are all in hopes that, yesterday and today, we have been having an earnest [view] of what we may yet behold in this part of the world — a rich, well-timbered, and sufficiently watered country.[26]

Such was the description of the area the Indians called *tonlt'ili,* meaning "where crystal water flows out." Here at the west entrance to Washington Pass, the only east-west corridor through the Chuska Mountains, lies the post of Crystal.[27] Blessed with a rare combination of beautiful red-rock buttes, interspersed with mountain greenery, the location was long a favored Indian campsite — but not in winter. "The mountain plain was very pleasant in summer," wrote Thomas Keam to Interior Secretary Henry M. Teller in 1884, "but entirely impracticable in winter, as it is one of the coldest places on the reservation. [I] was told that eighteen inches of snow fell there on the last of April. Whoever recommended [location of the sheep ranch] never visited the place in winter when it is often covered with two feet of snow."[28]

The success of early Navajo trading ventures did not generally include mountain bases. The seasonal handicaps were just too harsh. Some operations did well in summer when herders brought their flocks to graze the high country meadows, but deep snows which lay from October to late spring usually meant disaster. Several made a run at it though, including Archibald Sweetland who sat out many a lonely hour in a log post called Schili,

Schili Trading Post, 1890.

Archibald Sweetland (fourth from left) poses in the compound at his stockade-type post high in the Chuska timbers. Late Classic Period stripes and bands are prevalent in the displayed fabrics, as well as a Mexican-Saltillo, serrated diamond-designed rug in the center. Note the dangling price tags, indicating that some sales force was in place. The man at the right is wearing a popular Chief Blanket shoulder wrap of the period. If color was imagined, this piece would be a striking cloth of bright bayeta red (respun cloth) fashioned with broad bands of red, white and indigo blue checks. One interesting aspect of the photograph, recorded near the turn of the century, shows rugs that represent pre-Bosque Redondo designs and styles (1850-1863). While appearing to be well-woven products, the unbordered motifs were not in the mainstream of other weaving areas at that time (i.e., brightly colored Germantown and Saxony textiles). Perhaps the remoteness of Schili and its area weavers inhibited change and innovative techniques. *Photo courtesy of Museum of New Mexico.*

Inside the store, 1911. John B. Moore (facing camera, on left) beside manager, Jesse A. Molohon. *Reproduced from* The Navajo, *1911. Courtesy of Gallup, New Mexico Public Library.*

In front of the trading post, 1911. Manager Molohon holding Indian child; Moore, second from right. *Reproduced from* The Navajo, *1911. Courtesy of Gallup, New Mexico Public Library.*

tition in them. There is just one BEST quality, and that is the J.B. MOORE rugs, woven exclusively for him by the Crystal, N. Mex. colony of Navajo weavers. Our ewavers are better paid than any others, but they do better work and that is WHY they do it. Our finest rugs may be higher priced than those of some others, but they are finer and better woth their price. And, you cannot get their equal from any other at any price, unless it may be from someone who first bought them here.

You are not asked or expected to accept my bare statement for this. See the goods and then decide. I will ship on approval and if you are not wholly satisfied ship back at my expense. This is the kind my rugs are. I gladly take all risk of return expense for the chance of having you see them. A satisfied customer is worth more to me than any one sale. At least, they will not turn away from me friends who may want similar goods.

In 1911, shortly after publishing his catalog, Moore sold his holdings to his manager of three years, Jesse A. Molohon.[30] From 1919 to 1922, the post was in the store chain of Gallup businessman, C.C. Manning. Manning's clerk, Charlie Newcomb, was an owner until 1936, followed by Jim Collyer (1936-1944) and Don Jensen (1944-1981). Al Townsend owned the post for five years before moving north to Inscription House Trading Post, selling out to Charlie and Evelyn Andrews in 1986.

The Rug

The early *Crystal* rug of Moore's design was a bordered product designed with crosses, diamonds, terraces, a characteristic hook and fork pattern (Greek frets), along with swastikas and arrows. The Moore line was generously embellished with aniline red and to lesser degrees, outlines of blue.

Crystal Area Map

20-Year Comparative Costs					Weavers
Year	**3' x 5'**	**4' x 6'**	**6' x 9'**	**Large Specials**	Amos Begay
1978	$200-350	$600-750	$800-1,200	$1,500+	Margaret Begay
1988	$400-600	$800-1,000	$1,500-2,000	$3,500+	Mary T. Begay
1998	$700-2,000	$2,500-5,000	—	—	Rachel Begay
					Irene Clark
					Timothy Livingston
Trading Posts		**Traders**			Mary T. Moore
					Ella Rose Perry
Crystal Trading Post		Charlie & Evelyn Andrews			Lydia Peshlakai
					Jennett Tsosie
					Mary Wingate

canyon, although the Navajos themselves may have set fire to them as they fled. Following this, in 1864, Kit Carson's troops arrived during the bitterly remembered "Navajo roundup".

The deep, thousand-foot chasms of the canyon offered protection; the bottomlands served as excellent farms; the juniper and piñon-forested rims yielded timber and fuel; and the soil permitted limited grazing. The canyon has been sparsely occupied from about 1300 A.D. until arrival of the Navajo in the region (1600 A.D.). It was a natural site for trade purposes.

The first known merchant was a non-licensed trader that the Navajos called Naakaii Yazzie ("Little Mexican"), who operated out of a tent in 1882 at an undetermined location near Chinle.[35] The first permanent operation was established by Hubbell and his partner, C. N. Cotton, in 1885.[36] Their site was an abandoned rock hogan, which in later years became the location of Garcia's Trading Post. The enterprise soon failed when, for alleged political reasons, their application for a license was denied. However, several licensed traders soon followed Hubbell and Cotton at the rock hogan location: Michael Donovan (1887), Thomas J. Lingle (1888), Bernard J. Mooney and James F. Boyle (1889) and John W. Boehm (1889).

In 1900, Hubbell returned to Chinle and constructed a second post on a rocky knob of land approximately one mile west of his original store.[37] Realizing the scenic potential of Canyon de Chelly, Hubbell built a two-story, fortress-style, rock hotel to accommodate guests, with the floor level serving as the trading post. Hubbell's foresight for tourism was perceptive, but it was 30 years premature. The poor travel conditions on the reservation at that time resulted in few tourists and therefore a disappointing business.

In 1902, Samuel E. Day moved in and built a log store a short distance south of the mouth of Canyon de Chelly.[38] This store, a forerunner of the existing Thunderbird Lodge, was referred to by the Navajos as *aa dee kin ye*, simply meaning, "the big house over there." In 1905, Day sold out to Charles F. Weidemeyer who ran the post for 11 years before transferring ownership to George Kennedy in 1916.

Garcia Trading Post, 1926. *Reproduced from* Navajo Trading Days, *Hegemann, 1963. Courtesy of University of New Mexico Press.*

Plate 20
Chinle (36" X 44")
Weaver: Unknown
Source: Courtesy of Hubbell Trading Post, Ganado, Arizona (C. 1970)
Construction: Partly synthetic dyed, partly vegetal dyed, all handspun.

Considering its traditional environs, Chinle was a desirable trading region, but not quite large enough to support three posts with Boehm, Hubbell and Kennedy not realizing much profit from the divided business. The situation improved in 1923 when a tri-partnership of Camille Garcia (a former Hubbell clerk), Leon H. "Cozy" McSparron and Hartley T. Seymour bought the properties. They closed down Hubbell's old sandstone "castle" and concentrated their business back at the two sites near the mouth of the canyon. Garcia eventually assumed sole ownership of the original 1885 Hubbell site (rock hogan) and operated a successful trading business there until its closure in late 1985.

Similarly, McSparron bought out Seymour's interest in the old Day post in 1925. He renamed the place Thunderbird Lodge, and with Canyon de Chelly National Monument soon to be established (April 1, 1931), added guest accommodations and achieved Hubbell's earlier dream — a lucrative tourist business. McSparron held sway for nearly 30 years, building a reputation as a master host, reputable trader and promoter of Navajo weaving. "Cozy" retired to Sedona, Arizona, in 1954, and sold his interests to John Nelson, who continued the dual trader/tourist operation. Following Nelson's death five years later, his widow managed the post until 1964, when the facility was purchased by Gerald LaFont, who slowly phased out the trading business, concentrating wholly on tourism.

The Rug

Trader Leon H. "Cozy" McSparron, his wife, Inja, and patron of Navajo arts Mary C. Wheelwright, are responsible for the *Chinle* rug style.[39] Their experiments in the 1930s with vegetal dyes provided impetus to area weavers to revive the simple stripes and bands of the Classic Period. The *Chinle* rug has maintained this basic suggestion, and while generally considered to be primarily vegetal, synthetic dyes were later used to accentuate the smaller designs.

Salina Trading Post, 1987.

The borderless rug has a spacious feeling with small terraced designs and squash blossoms encased in broad bands. Some of the intervening stripes use the *Crystal* "wavy line" technique. The weavers in the district create an attractive rug of pleasing balance. Natural white wool usually provides the background, with lesser used shades of vegetal-dyed green, brown and gray. Rose colors and yellows are favorites, along with commercial dyes to denote outlines and termination panels on the ends. The rug is distinctive and well woven. Some of the better pieces must be closely examined to distinguish them from a *Crystal* or a *Wide Ruins*. One of the keys is dye utilization: part vegetal and part synthetic. Also, the weave is somewhat heavier than its all-vegetal neighbors. Today, there is a trend developing in the modern *Chinle* rug toward more use of pastel-colored commercial yarn.

A small trading post called Nazlini, located 20 miles south of Chinle, prompted a few arguments among rug experts in the 1960s. Some writers felt at that time that Nazlini area weavers wove a style that was distinctive enough to warrant regional recognition. The rug, known as the "Nazlini," was in essence an unbordered *Ganado*, exhibiting a combination of vegetal dyes and commercial colorants, particularly red. Prior to 1950, weavers of the district produced rugs exclusively in the Ganado style (red-black-gray-white). Some sources credit a missionary named Goss with influencing the Nazlini weavers to take up vegetal dyeing. The end result is that the so-called "Nazlini," being located halfway between Chinle and Ganado, actually reflects the style and colors of both areas in a pleasing combination. The basic design, however, is more aligned with *Chinle* characteristics.

Sam Day to

1902
Courtesy of Museum of New Mexico.

1938
National Park Service, courtesy of Fred Patton.

1944
Courtesy of Sallie Wagner.

Thunderbird Lodge

1951
Courtesy of Museum of New Mexico.

1987

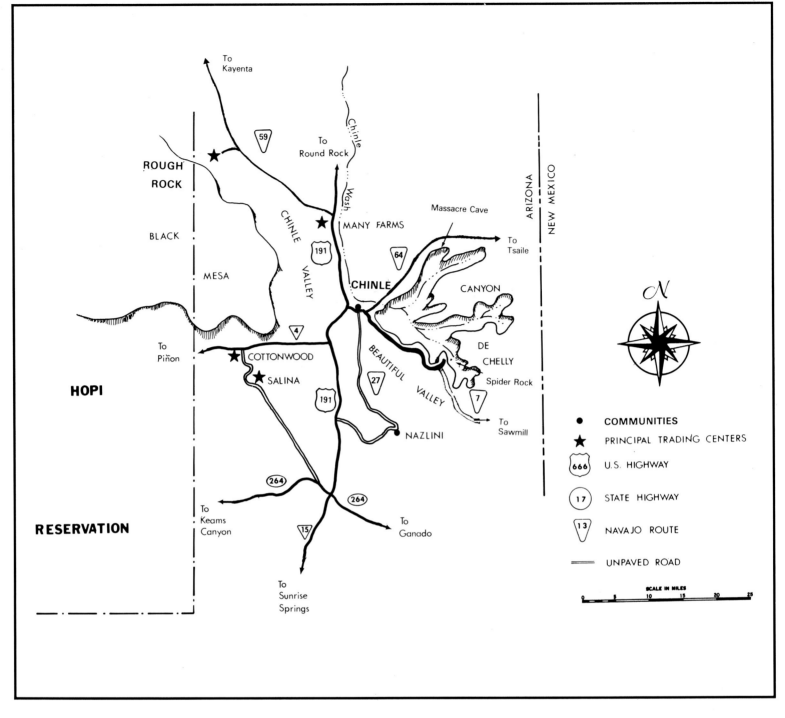

Chinle Area Map

20-Year Comparative Costs					Weavers
Year	**3' x 5'**	**4' x 6'**	**6' x 9'**	**Large Specials**	Jessie Gorman
					Ason Tsosie Hayou
					Rita Hayou
1978	$75-150	$250-350	$400-600	$1,000+	Suzie Hunter
1988	$250-400	$500-650	$750-1,000	—	Loren Nez
1998	$500-1,000	$1,200-3,000	—	—	Lana Spencer
					Elisabeth Stewart
					Sarah Van Winkle
Trading Posts		**Traders**			Ella Yazzie
					Rose Yazzie
Cottonwood Trading Post		Ernest Gormon			
Many Farms Trading Post		Claire Allison			
Rough Rock Trading Post		Al Grieve			
Salina Trading Post		Dave Murray			

Chapter 9

GANADO
'Home of a Trading Empire'

Hubbell Trading Post from the top of Hubbell Hill, 1972.

J. L. Hubbell, *Courtesy of Museum of New Mexico.*

Hubbell Residence, 1890
Backdropped by conical-shaped Hubbell Hill, this dwelling was built by W.B. Leonard about 1875. It was situated directly north of the trading post on the banks of Pueblo Colorado Wash. Hubbell (standing by tree), later built a larger, more comfortable home directly behind the store in 1900. The second Hubbell residence, which can be visited today, hosted scores of guests during his occupancy, including visits by President Theodore Roosevelt in 1913 and 1915. *Photo courtesy of Museum of New Mexico.*

The Post

There was an aura of history and permanence about Ganado [Hubbells] that no other trading post could achieve. It was not only the long dim store with high counters, whose only light came through two barred windows at the front, it was memories of other times (Hegemann, 1963).

Ganado is situated on the crimson shale plains midway between the Defiance Plateau on the east and the Hopi mesas to the west. The main trading center is nestled in a small valley along the southern banks of Pueblo Colorado Wash, 35 miles south of Chinle.

The first settlement in the area dates back to at least Basketmaker III Period around the 8th century, and possibly even earlier. Ancestors to some of the Hopi Indians probably occupied a communal dwelling nearby called Wide Reeds in the 13th century. The first trading post, called Pueblo Colorado (Spanish for "Red Village"), was established by Charles Crary in 1871. William B. "Old Man" Leonard also traded in the area between the years 1876-1878 before selling out to Juan Lorenzo Hubbell.[40] Hubbell, in honor of his friend and Navajo headsman, Ganado Mucho (Spanish for "Many Cattle"), is responsible for the current place name. From this headquar

Hubbell Warehouse, 1890
A youthful looking Juan Lorenzo (far left) poses with employees amidst a clutter of goods of the period. From left to right, some identifiable items include: bales of hay, bundles of wool, rugs, crates of Arbuckles Coffee, Dukes Mixture Tobacco, Gold Medal Flour and on the far right, what appears to be sacks of grain. From the rafters drip stalactites of hides, harness and tack, saddles, ropes, brooms, a bird cage and a baby buggy: a varied lot, indicative of the necessities of successful trading. *Photo courtesy of Museum of New Mexico.*

Hubbell Complex, 1904
View is south across Pueblo Colorado Wash. From left to right the structures are: (1) the first Leonard home, (2) multiple-windowed, north facade of trading post, (3) large, porch-fronted second Hubbell home, (4) massive-constructed warehouse, (5) storage shed and/or employee's quarters. Note white-washed privy sitting precariously on the stream bank in middle ground. *Photo courtesy of Museum of New Mexico.*

The Home

The Bullpen

ters, Hubbell, who briefly held a partnership with C. N. Cotton, built a trading empire which eventually encompassed 24 trading posts, wholesale warehousing, stage lines and freighting. His reputation gained the title, "the greatest of all Indian traders."[41] Hubbell managed his vast holdings for over 50 years. When he died on November

The Rug Room

12, 1930, responsibility for the property was assumed by his son, Roman, who carried on until his death in October, 1957. His wife, Dorothy, continued the family managership until 1967. Hubbell Hill, a conical-shaped promontory north of the post, serves as the family cemetery plot, bearing the remains of Lorenzo, Sr., his wife, Lina Rubi; two sons, Lorenzo, Jr., and Roman; a daughter, Adele; and Many Horses, a Navajo family friend.

On April 3, 1967, Hubbell Trading Post was purchased by the federal government to be operated as a National Historic Site. It is an installation that functions largely in the manner which warranted its preservation — trading with the Indians. Today, guides conduct regular tours through the old Hubbell home, the post and surrounding grounds. Under National Park Service management, Southwest Parks and Monuments Association operates the post as a living history museum— a trading post carrying on the old tradition so well exemplified by Juan Lorenzo Hubbell.[42]

The Post

Plate 23
Ganado (36"
X 42")
Weaver: Unknown
Source: Courtesy of Hubbell
Trading Post, Ganado, AZ (1973)
Construction: Mostly synthetic
dyed, processed white, all
handspun.

Plate 24
Ganado (36" x 42")
Weaver: Unknown
Source: Courtesy of Hubbell
Trading Post (1973)
Construction: Mostly synthetic
dyed, processed white, all
handspun.

Plate 25
Ganado (36" X 42")
Weaver: Unknown
Source: Courtesy of Hubbell
Trading Post, Ganado, AZ (1973)
Construction: Mostly synthetic
dyed, natural carded gray, all
handspun.

Plate 26
Ganado
(20" X 40")
Weaver:
Unknown
Source: Courtesy
of Burnham
Trading Post,
Sanders, AZ (1987)
Construction: All commercial
yarn.

The Rug

The famed "Ganado red" is perhaps the best known of all Navajo rugs, considered by most non-Indians what a Navajo rug should look like. Its creator, Juan Lorenzo Hubbell, possessed a philosophy that . . . *a good Navajo rug is like money in the bank.* He specialized in a well-woven product that featured a brilliant red background surrounded by strong geometric crosses, diamonds and stripes constructed with yarns of gray, white, and black. Hubbell's influence is still very much in evidence in the modern *Ganado.* The central motif is usually a bold diamond or cross, mostly outlined in another color. Smaller forms occupy the remaining spaces. The rug can range from large, simple, bold designs to intricate, more sophisticated works. The deep red is still the dominant force throughout the fabric, although recently the tones have taken on rich shades of burgundy. In some contemporary examples, various shades of gray are replacing the red backgrounds. The average *Ganado,* while usually of area size, has a modern-day tendency to feature smaller tapestry types for wall hangings.

Although areas to the south are primarily vegetal-dye centers, the *Ganado* is a combination of natural colors (grays and whites), with synthetic dyes of black and the characteristic deep, rich red.

Two areas identified with the *Ganado,* but sometimes subdivided into separate regional style centers, are Piñon to the west and Klagetoh to the south. The familiar red-black-gray-white influence is evident in both. In contemporary weaves, however, neither Klagetoh nor Piñon has achieved the individualism to warrant regional style recognition. Weavers in the Piñon—Keams Canyon area during the Revival Period became famous for their huge

loom products, one measuring as much as 24 x 36 feet. Some rug experts felt that this size trait was sufficient to separate Piñon from the rest of the styles. However, in comparing early *Ganado* rugs, large sizes were also one of the chief characteristics.

From the Klagetoh "namers" comes further confusion. Located 12 miles south of Ganado, Klagetoh Trading Post achieved some measure of publicity during the 1960s from retailers calling a certain type of *Ganado,* a "Klagetoh." Here, the same red-black-gray-white rug prevails. Some current arguments insist that the "Klagetoh" is more sophisticated than the *Ganado;* that there is more design and complication in the pattern and elimination of Late Classic Period crosses and diamonds; the use of less red, more gray (particularly as a background color) and the prevalence of serrated borders. Carelessness in rug naming continued farther when even the "Klagetoh" was subdivided. Twenty miles to the west, a post called Sunrise Springs found itself named in recognition of a particular serrated diamond-type rug — the "Klagetoh Sunrise." In all cases, the final answer was from the imaginative mind of Juan Lorenzo Hubbell. His influence on Navajo weaving styles touched a greater geographic sphere than was originally considered.

In the 1970s, far to the north at the gateway to Monument Valley, some Kayenta weavers were producing excellent red-black-gray-white rugs in typical *Ganado* designs. Some writers, or enterprising retailers, were apparently attempting to devise a new regional style rug to be called a "Kayenta". The only differing trait in the rug was its white background (instead of red and gray) and smaller designs. It never caught on.

Plate 27
Ganado (26" x 38")
Weaver: Bessie James
Source: Courtesy of Hubbell Trading Post,
Ganado, AZ (1987)
Construction: All commercial yarn.

Plate 28
Ganado (36" X 60")
Weaver: Unknown
Source: Courtesy of Burnham Trading
Post, Sanders, AZ (1987)
Construction: All commercial yarn.

Ganado Area Map

20-Year Comparative Costs				Weavers
Year	**3' x 5'**	**4' x 6'**	**6' x 9'**	**Large Specials**	Mary Lee Begay

20-Year Comparative Costs					Weavers
Year	**3' x 5'**	**4' x 6'**	**6' x 9'**	**Large Specials**	Mary Lee Begay
					Sadie Begay
					Beth Bitsoni
1978	$250-400	$500-750	$800-1,500	$2,000+	Evelyn Curley
1988	$500-750	$800-1,200	$1,500-2,500	$2,500+	Lucy James
1998	$1,500-2,000	$3,000-7,500	$7,500-12,000	$12,000+	Mary Jones
					Helen Kirk
Trading Posts		**Traders**			Mary Reed
					Harriet Smiley
Hubbell Trading Post (Ganado)		Bill Malone			Patsy Roan Horse
Keams Canyon Trading Post		Bruce McGee			Darlene Yazzie
Piñon Trading Post		Ferron McGee			
Steamboat Rock Trading Post		Jerrold B. Foutz			

Chapter 10

WIDE RUINS
'In the Hill Country of the Anasazi'

Wide Ruins Trading Post, 1973.

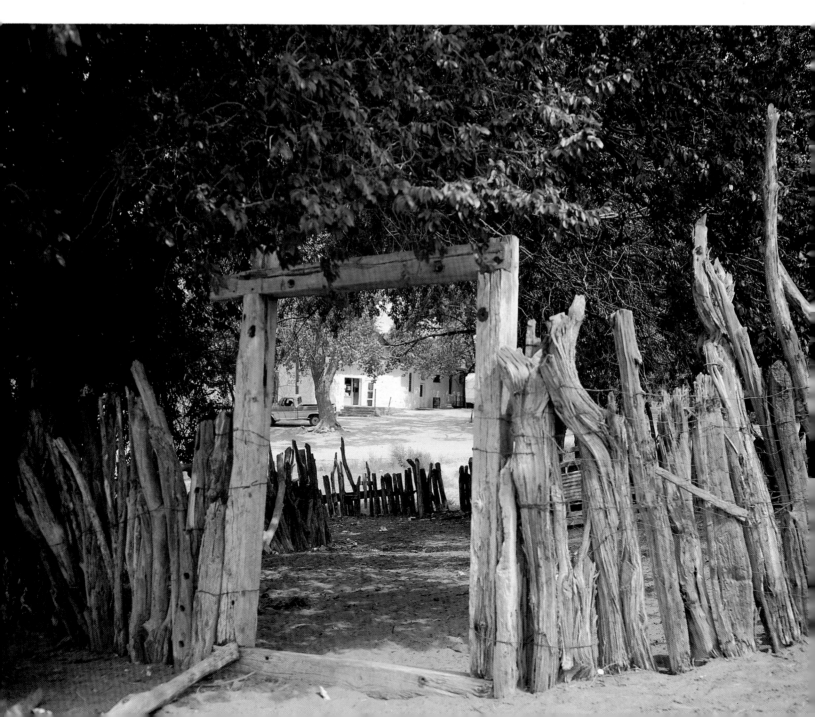

The Post

The trading center called Wide Ruins, named for the great Anasazi ruin, Kinteel, which means "Broad House", was located in the sage-covered hill country separating the Chinle Valley from the Rio Puerco.[43]

Stillness best describes the location. The buildings were situated off the main paved road and nestled in a sandy hillock that was hidden from the casual view by the low arms of spreading elm and cottonwood trees. Several, normally dry washes have carved colorful rocky swaths downhill from where the sheep corral stood and served as dividing lines separating the site from a more modern community and school on a hilltop to the northwest.

The Wide Ruins post was relatively new in the role of a rug center. Improved north-south roads connecting U.S. Highway 66 with paralleling reservation routes were mainly responsible for a series of 20th century trade centers that sprang up in between. At Kinteel, however, trading dates back to post-Bosque Redondo days, where a list of now-forgotten, transient entrepreneurs conducted their barters.[44]

The first permanent post, built of slab sandstone, was reportedly constructed by Sam Day (later of Chinle fame), probably around 1895. Whether Day actually traded at this location has not been established. The original post was built directly on the mound heaps of the Anasazi ruin, which occupied both sides of a small tributary of Wide Ruins Wash.[45]

The trading area was enclosed in a fortress-type compound constructed of logs and tree branches. In 1902, another larger rock store was built on the opposite (north) banks of the wash where it remained in varying modifications for 80 years.

The recordable succession of traders began in the early 1900s with the names of Spencer Balcomb, Wallace Sanders and Peter Paquette. Perhaps the name most associated with Wide Ruins is Lippincott. Bill Lippincott and his wife, Sallie, both recent graduates from the University of Chicago, spent the summer of 1938 as seasonal employees with the National Park Service at Canyon de Chelly. Succumbing to the love of the reservation, the Lippincotts began to search for an endeavor that would extend their stay. With the assistance and urging of Chinle neighbor, "Cozy" McSparron, they scouted the Indian country for a trading post to buy. In October of 1938, they closed a deal with former Navajo Commissioner, Peter Paquette, for what was then called Kinteel Trading Post. The complex sat on 160 acres of deeded land, which the Lippincotts had secured.

The Lippincotts deserve the credit for improving and publicizing the rug industry in the southeast corner of the reservation. Their insistence on the use of vegetal dyes and encouragement of quality weaving ultimately resulted in a superior textile. Sallie kept on hand a plant recipe book which weavers could consult; Bill promoted

a two-room addition to a nearby schoolhouse so that weaving classes could be taught to the younger women — promising to buy their class projects; and jointly, they conceived the idea of holding craft festivals which they hosted in their home, complete with refreshments, home movies, gifts for the children, and awards for the best weaving and silversmithing (Hannum, 1958).

Except for an absence during World War II, when Bill served as a naval commander in San Diego, the popular Lippincotts traded at Wide Ruins until August of 1950, when they sold out to the Navajo tribe.[46] A few years later the Foutz family assumed ownership, and the post was operated by Phil Foutz under the banner of Progressive Mercantile. Jim Collyer, Jr., son of the former Crystal trader, took over in 1957, followed by a partnership in 1964 when John Rieffer bought in. In July, 1973, the former sold out his interests, and the final owners, John and Sharon Rieffer, continued to promote weaving excellence.

Wide Ruins Vicinity Map

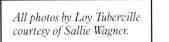

All photos by Loy Tuberville courtesy of Sallie Wagner.

Photo Album

Remains of original post, winter, 1946

Second store, built in 1902

Sallie and weaver

First stockade post, 1906

Outside the store, craft day, 1945

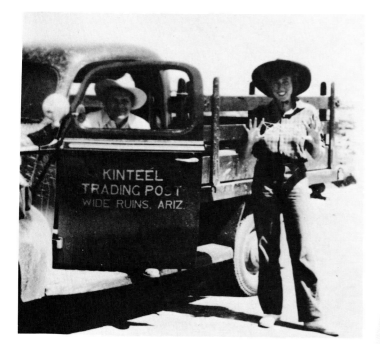

Bill and Sallie, 1945

Post from the south, 1941

Inside the store, 1944
Jean and Bill Cousins on the left (managers), Bill and Sallie facing camera

Remains of Wide Ruins Trading Post, 1987

Chapter 12

NEW LANDS
'A New Beginning'

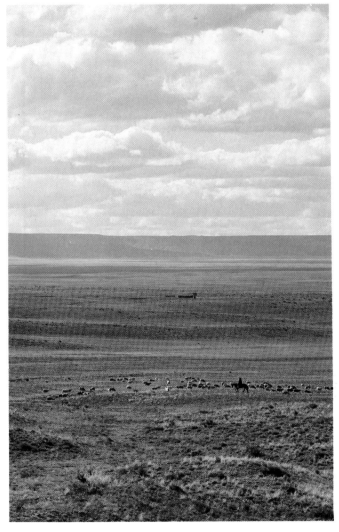

Herding on new lands.

Historical Development

Coal Mine Mesa is located on the Hopi Indian Reservation about 25 miles southeast of Tuba City, Arizona. A rug of the same name, which carried a raised outline feature, enjoyed a brief period of regional style recognition in the 1950s and early 1960s. Developed by the late Ned Hatathi as a Navajo Arts and Crafts Guild project, the textile represents more of a weaving technique than a style piece.[52] Through a manipulation of the weft and warp threads, various selected patterns can be slightly raised, and when outlined in a contrasting color, gives the design a three-dimensional effect.[53] Also, the raised outline appears on only one side, thus giving the rug the distinction of having a front and back surface. Through the intervening years, the raised outline technique has spread to other parts of the reservation, and coupled with the closing of the trading post at Coal Mine Mesa in 1968, the regional influence of the style was lost. The weave has remained popular, however, even into the modern era where it has prevailed as a specialty rug, and at times has been incorporated into other styles (i.e., "raised outline *Yei*", "raised outline *Storm Pattern*"; *see* Additional Notes 52, 53).

In the wake of the Navajo-Hopi Land Dispute, many Navajo families were relocated to other parts of the reservation.[54] This included 500 families who were resettled on new lands (hence the name) recently purchased by the tribe, south and east of Sanders, Arizona (*see* Burnt Water area map).[55] In 1982, principally through the promotions of Bruce Burnham at Sanders, Bill Malone of Hubbell Trading Post and Bruce McGee at Keams Canyon, the *Raised Outline* rug has resurfaced through the efforts of former Coal Mine Mesa weavers and has manifested itself into an entirely new style. Called *New Lands*, its evolution is born of combinations and techniques borrowed from other types, which is acceptable as the success of Navajo weaving has always depended on the flexibility to adapt and combine other innovations.

Plate 39
New Lands (36" X 48")
Weaver: Brenda Nez
Source: Courtesy of
Burnham Trading Post,
Sanders, Arizona (1987)
Construction: All vegetal-
dyed commercial yarn.

Plate 38
New Lands (30" X 48")
Weaver: Lavern Yazzie
Source: Courtesy of Burnham Trading Post,
Sanders, Arizona (1987)
Construction: All vegetal-dyed commercial yarn.

The Rug

The *New Lands* is basically a composite textile of *Teec Nos Pos* designs that is constructed of vegetal-dyed commercial yarn and features the raised outline technique. Being vegetal, its palate is soft pastels and differs in that respect from the brightly colored, parent rug of the Four Corners area. It is extremely popular at this time, due principally to its limited production, excellent weave, design appeal and decorator colors, as well as featuring the desirable raised outline. Because of its newness, it is also receiving attention at arts and crafts shows, from museum procurers, dealers and collectors. Some *Burntwater* designs are also being constructed in the raised outline format, but because of fewer geometrics required in the design, are less expensive. Only time and the demand of "aficionados" will determine and judge the future of the *New Lands* raised outline.

20-Year Comparative Costs				Weavers
Year **3' x 5'**	**4' x 6'**	**6' x 9'**	**Large Specials**	Andrew Begay
1978 —	—	—	—	Keith Begay
1988 $2,000-3,500	$4,500-7,000	$8,500-12,000	$15,000+	Mary Begay
1998 $3,000-4,000	$6,000-8,000	$15,000-18,000	$20,000+	Stanley Begay
				Wanda Begay
Trading Post		**Trader**		Sarah Tsinnie
Burnham Trading Post		Bruce Burnham		Janet Tsinnie
(Sanders, Arizona)				

Chapter 13

WESTERN RESERVATION

Plate 40
Storm Pattern, raised
outline (32" X 50")
Weaver: Rose Black
Mountain, Kayenta,
Arizona
Source: Courtesy of
Bob French,
Waterflow, New
Mexico (1987)
Construction: All
commercial yarn.

Winter silhouette, Monument Valley, 1972.

Red Lake
'On the Rainbow Trail'

The Post

The Red Lake Trading Post at *Tonalea*, Navajo meaning "Where Water Comes Together", is said to be the birthplace of the reservation's most controversial and interestingly designed rug — the *Storm Pattern*.

Situated halfway down the slope of a sandy mesa, with environs strongly resembling a desert of the Far East, the trading post was named for a shallow expanse of land that is only a "lake" during wet years. The best thing about Red Lake, and it is argumentative, is the view to the east where Black Mesa breaks the rather desolate, unattractive foreground. Rattlesnakes thrived and loved the place. Trader Johnny O'Farrell (1918-1935) killed them by the hordes during spring and summer months. Johnny's wife, Cora, gained more than a local reputation by serving her "special tuna sandwiches" to passing tourists. It was said that she always enjoyed watching the visitors gag a bit, when told it was freshly boiled rattlesnake meat. Equally interesting was Cora's favorite piece of jewelry — a threaded necklace of a rattlesnake's spinal column.

Red Lake Trading Post was established in 1881, in the northwest corner of the Hopi Reservation, by Joseph H. Lee, son of John Doyle Lee of Lee's Ferry fame. The post was situated at two different sites prior to its final location. Lee's original store, a canvas-topped shack, was two miles down the wash to the southwest. In 1885, George McAdams moved the store back to the east, along the south shore of the "lake". In 1888, McAdams sold out to a Dutchman named Dittenhoffer. "Ditt," as he was called, was killed in a lover's quarrel at the post in 1890. His principal creditor, Charles Babbitt of Babbitt Brothers Trading Company of Flagstaff, Arizona, assumed active control of the post a year later and moved the operation to its present rock-constructed, two-story quarters in 1891.[56]

The post functioned as a company-operated enterprise. Babbitt Brothers, who owned a chain of trading posts on the Navajo and Hopi reservations, initiated their business through a resident manager-trader arrangement with partnership privileges. Beginning in 1891, with a first manager named Sam Preston, the succession of em

The desert setting of Red Lake Trading Post at Tonalea, 1949. View is south across dried-up lake flats toward Black Mesa on the horizon. *Photo courtesy of Museum of New Mexico.*

Plate 41
Storm Pattern, raised outline (32" x 58")
Weaver: Unknown
Source: Private collection (1972)
Construction: Partly synthetic dyed, natural carded gray, all handspun.

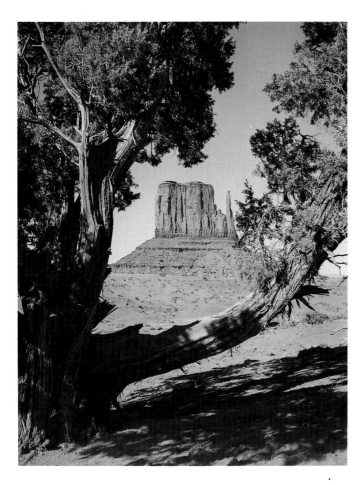

West Mitten, Monument Valley.

ployees has been: H.K. Warren (1897-1905), Earl Boyer (1905-1918), Johnny O'Farrell (1918-1935), Floyd Boyle (1935-1953), Coit Patterson (1953-1955), Harold Lockhart (1955-1973), and Jerry Norris (1973-1987).[57]

One of the more interesting sidelights to the old post was the periodic visits of the noted author, Zane Grey. Grey, seemingly quite taken with the northwest corner of the Indian country, was the guest of trader Earl Boyer on several occasions between 1911-1914, while gathering material for the *Rainbow Trail* (1915). The first chapter of the book is set at Red Lake Trading Post.

The Rug

The basic design of the *Storm Pattern* is a bordered rug that is highly symmetrical, displaying certain standard features. Always there is a square or rectangular center from which radiating lines lead to the four corners, where additional squares are set. Secondary elements may include zigzags, diamonds, arrows and stepped terraces serving as fillers along the borders. The rug tends to be elongated in shape to facilitate connecting lines between the rectangular designs. Weavers of the *Storm Pattern* work primarily in commercial dyes of red-black-gray-white combinations.

The contemporary *Storm Pattern*, although still very much in evidence in western sectors, is now being found throughout the reservation. Beautiful examples are woven in most areas and sometimes display characteristics of the local regional style. Even vegetal-dyed *Storm Patterns* can be found on racks.[58]

The origin of the *Storm Pattern* has prompted considerable debate. The general inclination is to consider it symbolic, although the symbolism appears to have been conceived by a white man. The traditional sales factor in describing the alleged "sacredness" of the rug is that the center square is the hogan, or "center of the world," and that the four squares at each of the corners represent the four sacred mountains of Navajo mythology.[59] The connecting lines, usually zigzagged, are intended as lightning bolts carrying blessings back and forth between the squares, thereby delivering good spirits on the weaver's household.

Some writers credit an early trader with creating the *Storm Pattern* design. Others say that it is a variation of a commercial design that appeared on flour sacks being shipped out of Flagstaff at the turn of the century. In *Navajo Trading Days*, Hegemann (1963) describes a rug that displays all of the standard features of a contemporary *Storm Pattern*. Her description reads:

> A typical and popular rug pattern woven in the district of Western Navajo between Kayenta and Tuba. Many of the good weavers of the Tsayutcissi family used this design of the Four Mountains bordering the Navajo World with the lake in the middle, and the Sacred Arrows, and Whirling Logs. This was called the Red Lake pattern because a trader at that post had originated the design sometime after 1900. *Courtesy of University of New Mexico Press.*

Another possibility would seem to rest with the imagination of John B. Moore of Crystal. Moore was continually involved with design innovations. Pictured in his mail order catalog, *The Navajo* (1911), is a perfect example of a modern-day *Storm Pattern*. Moore called this his ER-20 Class, "Special Design Rug," and noted that "...it is legendary in Navajo mythology and not many weavers will do it for superstitious reasons." Considering that passage, it would appear that Mr. Moore's design abilities were possibly exceeded by his salesmanship.

PLATE XXVIII

Special Design and Weave by "Dug-gau-eth-lun bi Dazhie."

From "ER-20" class, original 64x92 inches in size. This pattern is one of the really legendary designs embodying a portion of the Navajo mythology. Not many weavers will do it for superstitious reasons and on that account its production is practically confined to one family or clan. It is an improved adaptation of Plate IX, also originated by this same woman, and done in red, white and black. She, and her immediate relatives, have been making it as shown here for two or three years past, and the rug has never failed to satisfy when shown to a prospective buyer. The trouble has been to get enough of them made, and to overcome this is the main purpose of this engraving. With the pattern for a working model, we hope to get other weavers to making it.

"ER-20" class, size 45x75 inches up to 6x9 feet and price, 90c to $1.00 per square foot, or $21.00 to $23.50 for small, and up or down, according to size. Made to order in any size and colors desired at price in proportion to size, but the colors shown can hardly be improved upon.

Very rarely done in the "T-XX" class, but at $1.00 to $2.00 per lb., if we should chance to have any. Not made to order in this class.

John B. Moore's "Special Design Rug"— a forerunner to the modern-day Storm Pattern. *Reproduced from* The Navajo, *1911. Courtesy of Gallup, New Mexico Public Library.*

Above:
Plate 42
Storm Pattern (36" X 48")
Weaver: Unknown
Source: Courtesy of Hubbell Trading Post, Ganado, Arizona (1973)
Construction: Partly synthetic dyed, natural white, natural carded gray, all handspun.

Below:
Plate 43
Storm Pattern (24" X 36")
Weaver: Unknown
Source: Courtesy of Price's All Indian Shop, Albuquerque, New Mexico (1970)
Construction: Partly synthetic dyed, partly vegetal dyed, all handspun.

Shonto
'Place of Sunlight Water'

Shonto Trading Post, 1987.

Trader Trolet and family, 1987.

Shonto Trading Post, 1932. *Reproduced from* Navajo Trading Days, *Hegemann, 1963. Courtesy of University of New Mexico Press.*

The Post

The remote trading post of Shonto deserves some mention, for there is no other place on the Navajo Reservation that retains the traditional integrity of the early days of Indian trading as the *place in the canyon (see* title page sketch). A *primitive place* where few roads enter and, until a short time ago, only Navajo was the spoken language and trade goods were known by pictures on wrappers, not by printed labels. An *isolated place* where the nearest phone was 25 miles away and ponies and wagons were more valued and practical then pickup trucks. A *small place*, not ambitious in motive or attitude, where some traders could break even on a handful of daily customers, a few head of sheep, some good saddle blankets and an occasional bumper crop of piñon nuts. And finally, an *amazingly picturesque place* — a gem setting in the fall when gold leaves of the cottonwood grove contrast brilliantly against a backdrop of 200-foot salmon-pink cliffs.

First out of a tent, then a one-room rock store, Joe Lee developed the site in 1914 along the base of the east wall of Shonto Canyon — a ten-mile, non-river gorge that carries runoffs from snowmelts and summer thunderstorms. The post owes it existence to a bubbling spring, *a place of sunlight water* (its translated name), that proved dependable in a wilderness of sandstone.

Early automobile access was difficult, if not downright hazardous — six miles upstream through the mouth of the canyon; a trek that often required fighting a set of sand ruts going in and making your own coming out, and all the while keeping a wary eye out for cloudbursts. In 1930, when trader Harry Rorick blasted a dugway up the east face so archaeologists and tourists could more easily reach the cliff dwelling of Betatakin seven miles away, it

Shonto country.

was described as the "roughest damn half-mile in America" — it hasn't changed.

The unique post is in keeping with the people that it serves. The Navajos of the district have distinguished themselves for being the last stronghold of the "long hairs" — a traditional clan grouping that holds fast to the old ways. Today, these proud ones are the descendants of those who made a fighting retreat into the recesses of Navajo Mountain and escaped the "Long Walk" and misery of Bosque Redondo.

Western Reservation Area Map

20-Year Comparative Costs					Weavers	
Year	**3' x 5'**	**4' x 6'**	**6' x 9'**	**Large Specials**	Mary Begamble	Bessie Sellers
1978	$200-250	$300-400	$500-650	$1,000+	Lucille Begay	Susie Tacheene
1988	$300-500	$500-750	$1,000-2,000	$3,000+	Helen Bigman	Mary Tisi
1998	$1,000-2,500	$3,000-6,000	$6,000-10,000	$15,000+	Veronica Begay	Lily Touchin
					Lorinda Bennette	Lillie Nes Tsosi
					Mary Clark	
Trading Posts		**Traders**			Mary Fowler	
					Anna Grayhat	
Cedar Ridge Trading Post		Jerry Whiterock			Betty Ann Huskon	
Cow Springs Trading Post		Bennie Garcia			Leona Littleman	
Inscription House Trading Post		Al Townsend			Mary S. Nez	
Shonto Trading Post		Melissa and Ray Trolet			Shirley Nockidench	
The Gap Trading Post		Jim Wilson				
Tuba City Trading Post		Jerry Norris				

Chapter 14

SPECIALTY RUGS AND OTHER TYPES★

Monogram
Usually square and small in size, the *Monogram* rug can carry almost any message the weaver desires: people's names, places of business, patriotic slogans, etc.

Outline
The *Outline* rug features a multiple outlining of the designs in different colors. The rug is usually bordered, encasing a large central motif, such as a diamond or square.

Raised Outline
More of a weaving technique than a regional style piece, the *Raised Outline* is basically an outline rug that employs an edging weft of a different color to be transported over two warps instead of the customary one. This produces an elevated design outline on one surface of the rug (*see* Chapter 12; also Additional Notes 52, 53).

*Because these rug types are woven throughout the reservation, no differentiation is made as to preferences in wool/yarn usage, or dyes. It is inferred that a variety of methods and materials are utilized and employed in their construction.

Chief Blanket

Generally of small to moderate size, the modern-day *Chief*-designed rug is generally made of red, black, or dark-blue colored yarns, set in horizontal stripes, interspaced with bands of white or gray. Smaller design elements, such as checks, diamonds and crosses, may occupy the center and corner edges. The rug has lost the significance for which it was named (*see* Additional Note 8). Its design continues to live, however, because of the historical prestige it once enjoyed.

Pictorial

Amsden (1934), in discussing *Pictorial* rugs, says, "It is doubtful if any weaver ever attempted to draw a picture to tell a story upon her loom until after the American conquest. Now she launches forth ambitiously with flags and rampant eagles and square-wheeled railway cars."

As early as the late 1800s, Navajo weavers illustrated their textiles with pictures of animals and human forms. The *Pictorial* rug is woven in a variety of usually bright colors. Likewise, a variety of subject matter is displayed depending upon the fancy of the weaver — pickup trucks, hogans, mountains, animals (particularly horses, cattle and sheep) and people are all portrayed in a somewhat crowded manner.

Bird Rug

A type of a *Pictorial* rug that has endured from early-day graphics to the present, is a large, leafless tree with arrays of multiple-colored birds perched upon branches. The rug is generally small to moderate in size and usually without a border. Weavers in The Gap Trading Post area are noted for this particular type rug.

Monogram-Pictorial

Combining words with pictures on a rug is a relatively modern approach. An American flag with U.S.A. across the top, the name of a person, or the name of a trading post above a building, all add personal touches to a rug that often conveys more meaning to whom it is directed, rather than general appeal.

Hide Rug

A rare specialty of moderate size that depicts the skinned rawhide of a cow. An imaginative piece that is woven to clearly outline the reddish-brown body (complete with tail) and white markings of a skinned hide. Some examples are expertly done and from distant viewing remarkably resemble a rawhide surface.

Circular Rug

Another innovation that has emerged is a small rug which surfaced in 1971. Completely circular (usually 18" in circumference), it is woven in typical *Ganado* designs with red-black-gray-white colors. An air of intrigue surrounds the rug in as much as the weavers who accomplish this feat refuse to allow anyone to observe their technique or examine their loom. Some writers suspect a loom arrangement fashioned within the radius of a wagon wheel.

Sandpainting Rug

These rugs are woven copies, though not exact, of sandpainting designs. The rugs are light weight, unbordered and square in size (3' x 3', 5' x 5'). Backgrounds are usually tan with brighter, multiple colors composing the designs. The overall depictions, taken from actual sacred healing designs, are quite busy and intricate. The favorite subjects in modern-day rugs are the sandpaintings of the Whirling Log, Shooting Chant, Water Creatures and the Earth Creatures.

Tufted Weave

The *Tufted Weave* is an unusual rug not often found in contemporary weaving. In essence, it is a shag-type rug that is made by inserting long strands of Angora goat wool in the weft threads, making it a one-sided rug. It is of small irregular size and shape. In some instances, weavers use the piece as a cushion surface during weaving.

Two-Faced Rug

A difficult rug, the *Two-Faced* is actually a fabric in which the two sides display entirely different designs and colors. To achieve this, the weaver places the weft threads one behind the other, instead of the conventional placement with threads placed atop one another. The rug is rare and understandably expensive. Being doubled in thickness in a two-styles-in-one development, it is more often coarse-textured and heavy. The *Two-Faced* rug dates from the late 1880s. It has never been extremely popular, but because of its unique and novel construction, it is attractive for collectors.

Twills

The term *Twill* not only signifies a rug type, but also a style of weaving that is achieved through arrangement of the loom heddles. Amsden (1934) explains:

> Twilling is a constant diagonal progression of stitches produced by the regular alteration of the point of insertion of warp and weft. The plain weave, for example, uses but two sheds, permitting no alteration of this point; the result is a fabric of vertical ribs with one string of warp (commonly) as the core of each. Twilling on the other hand (as done by the Navajo), employs four sheds, controlled by three heddles and the shed rod, the heddle arrangement being calculated to throw each stitch of weft one warp string to the right or left of the one preceding it. The result is a fabric of diagonal rather than vertical ribs.

All *Twill* weaves are constructed by carrying the weft over more than one warp at a time, thus adding thickness (bulk) throughout the entire fabric. *Twill*-constructed rugs, because of the heavier texture, are popular and more suited as floor coverings and saddle blankets.

Basically there are three types of *Twill* design: (1) *Diamond Twill*, (2) *Braided Twill* (herringbone or diagonal), and (3) *Plain Twill*.

Double Weave

The term *Double Weave* is a *Twill* variation combining a *Braided Twill* alternated with a *Diamond Twill* that has the order of colors reversed on the two sides.

The pattern remains identical, but by alternating colors through the entire width of the sheds, the arrangement of color changes from one side to the other, but maintains the same mirrored position.

Saddle Blanket

The *Saddle Blanket* is the only Navajo textile woven today that the Indians use for a functional purpose. It comes in two sizes: single (30"x 30") and double (30" x 60"). The blanket is purposely coarse-woven to take hard wear beneath the saddle. The format is usually unbordered, featuring simple serration and stripe and band designs. Colors are mostly bright, particularly at the corners and ends. Tassels are sometimes incorporated at the four corners in the more elaborate pieces. *Twill* weaving is used quite often in developing the piece. Many people use the *Saddle Blanket* as a floor item, mainly because of it durability.

Four-In-One

One of the most complex and rarely attempted rug is the *Four-In-One* style. It consists of four equal quadrants enclosed in a bordered format. Each square contains a separate design, each different from the other three. Some *Four-In-One* rugs display pairs of squares; i.e., two *Sandpaintings* and two *Pictorials*, or variations of the same style. Still rarer is the multiple-paneled rug that may display numerous styles — a patchwork quilt-like motif. Another, more contemporary fabric, is a "rug within a rug" which presents one style encased within another style.

Gallup Throw

Referred to by some writers as a regional style rug, the *Gallup Throw* is actually a tourist curio item developed near Gallup during the 1930s for railroad passengers. Today it can be found woven in many places on the reservation.

Some novice weavers practice with the throw-type rug before attempting more difficult designs and weaves. It is a small, inexpensive, borderless runner or table-top piece, often possessing a cotton warp, which is usually left dangling as a one or two-inch fringe at the ends. The rug is commonly of bright colors. Designs are relatively simple: broad chevrons, stripes, stylized diamonds and some displaying the Yei figure.

Other Types

Woman's Dress

This fabric is not a rug, but represents still another example of a Navajo woven product. The style of the *Woman's Dress* dates from the earliest influences of Pueblo women on the Navajo mode of attire. Design of the Navajo *Woman's Dress* is different from the plain Pueblo style, in that the Puebloans utilized one piece that was of sufficient width to permit doubling. The Navajo *Woman's Dress* consists of two pieces of fabric of identical size and shape to be worn as front and back pieces. It is secured at the top and bottom, with long slits along the sides to allow for arm movement. There are no sleeves. Simple stripes and small design elements decorate the piece in synthetic colors of black, red and blue.

The piece still retains the basic early style and design of the past two centuries. Three large panels, with alternating blocks of color, comprise the overall presentation, with interspacings of smaller stripes and bands. Small geometrics, such as rows of diamonds or checks, usually decorate the top and bottom sections.

A smaller version of the *Woman's Dress*, appropriately called *Child's Dress*, occasionally finds its way into rug outlets. These are quite rare and are sought as collectors' items.

Cross

This fabric, though actually not a rug (in the truest sense), is more of a symbol of the Late Classic Period Moqui (Hopi) cross that was popularized in *Ganado* motifs. Not only depicted as a cross, but also woven in the cross shape, it is quite unusual and appeals particularly to the serious collector. Usually attempted in moderate sizes (2' x 2'), it is utilized mostly as a table-top feature, or as a striking wall hanging.

Miniatures

Gaining popularity as collector items, miniature weavings are quite unique in reduced replicas of the standard creation. They represent all of the regional styles (plus some specialties), and are constructed with a variety of natural wool, processed wool and commercial yarn, and utilize both synthetic and vegetal dyes. In the good to outstanding examples, the smaller the size (involving finer stitching), the higher the price — being regarded as diminutive pieces of fine art. They range in size from a postage stamp to several inches square. The Fort Defiance area is noted for miniature weavings.

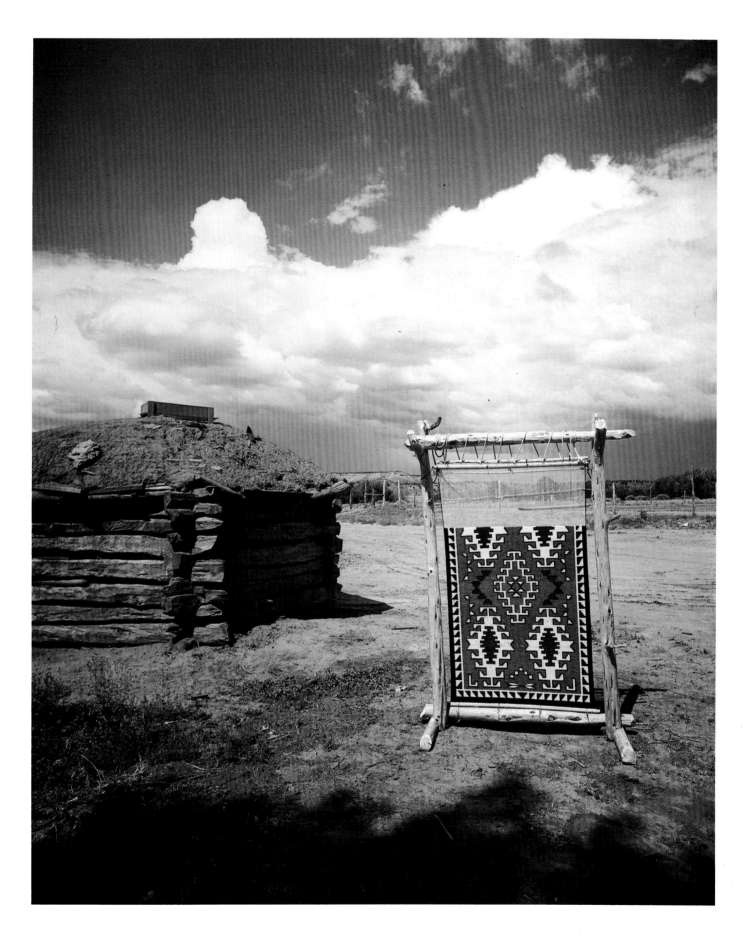

Standard Loom

A major woven product that is intact on a traditional log-constructed loom.
These dominant examples are rare and most are special ordered for specific
purposes; i.e., exhibits in museums and visitor's centers.

Miniature Loom

A popular novelty item, that is representative of an actual miniature rug woven on an actual miniature loom. Some come completely equipped with a spindle, fork, batten, tow cards, and shed and heddle rods. Most models stand 12" high and feature a variety of designs and dyes. The looms are very effective in publicizing Navajo weaving, particularly in an educational sense because the majority of non-Indians seldom witness the physical presence of a rug on a loom. In home decorating they pose an attractive visual display as mantle pieces.

Pillow-Top Covers

These woven covers add a distinction in contemporary home decorating. Their usage is somewhat limited, however, and are not always available, because it involves an off-reservation source for pillow manufacturing. Colors lack a broad range, leaning more toward the pastel shades to satisfy home color schemes. Designs are likewise simple and do not represent any regional style, but instead display uncomplicated patterns. Some *Yei*-designed pillow tops found in the Shiprock area are well done and present more of a traditional Navajo image.

General Rug

A fabric of almost any dimension, poor to excellent weave, featuring handspun, processed or commercial yarn, synthetic or vegetal-dyed, incorporating a multitude of designs, bordered or borderless. It may be woven in any locale on the reservation. The distinction of the general rug is that it does not possess sufficient characteristics to warrant recognition as a regional style rug or a specialty rug. The majority of rugs woven on the reservation today (40%) are in this category.

Special-Order Rug

Maxwell (1963) may have been in a whimsical mood when he suggested that anybody requiring a special order rug ... *should either learn to weave or marry a weaver*! True, a definite communication problem exists between weaver and customer. What may start out to be an understanding of size, color, dye and style invariably changes as the rug develops. Some weavers still sell their craft through their area trader, and understandably the trader is the only non-Indian who can suggest, influence, or commission for a certain type rug. The price for special-order rugs is usually quite high and the results almost always uncertain. Acquaintances made with traders and weavers on the reservation, however, can sometimes result in getting just what one ordered (*see Plate 9*).

Additional Notes

Chapter 1
History

The People

1. With the transfer of the Navajos back to their homeland, it was felt that Fort Wingate was too far removed from areas of resettlement to adequately assist in their supervision. General Getty explored the possibility of reestablishing the garrison further to the west. Fort Canby, which was abandoned after the "Navajo roundup" (October 8, 1864), would have been the ideal relocation site. The post, however, was in a state of complete ruin. Furthermore, being located 35 miles north of the main east-west road, it would have been economically unfeasible for the distribution of supplies and equipment. Getty decided, therefore, that the administration point would be established at Bear Springs and subsequently ordered the reactivation of Fort Lyon (old Fort Fauntleroy), but calling it the "new" Fort Wingate (James, 1967).

    As unforeseen by the government, the tendency for the Indians to gravitate toward the core of their *Dineth* (northwest to Canyon de Chelly), the further the distance became for the distribution of supplies from Fort Wingate. In the summer of 1868, the Bureau of Indian Affairs, under the guardianship of an agent, transferred their office to the ramshackled Fort Canby and restored its former name — Fort Defiance. The military, in a gesture of passive presence, remained at Fort Wingate.

The Traders

2. McNitt (1962, p.47n) reports that a few nomadic-type traders were licensed to patronize the Navajos in the early 1850s. Auguste LaComb, of French extraction, was granted a license in January 1853 — thus, being the earliest recorded Navajo trader.

3. Piñon, Spanish for "pine kernel" (called neschi by the Navajos), is an edible nut about the size of a small pea. It occurs in the cones of the brushy Piñon pine (Pinus edulis) at elevations of 6,000-8,000 feet. Along the reaches of the Chuska Mountains and Defiance Plateau on the east, and in western sectors of the Shonto high country, the piñon forests are thick, although bountiful crops only develop every 3-5 years. Those trading posts that were situated near these forested environs usually did a considerable business with this additional commodity. Harvested in the fall, the nuts were sacked in 90-pound bags and wholesaled out of Gallup, New Mexico, to be shipped to populous markets where they were cleaned, processed (salted), packaged and sold similar to peanuts. The *McKinley County Republican* reported on November 24, 1911, that one local wholesaler alone had contracted for 60,000 pounds of nuts, at five cents a pound. Kluckhohn and Leighton (1946) stated that one trader in 1936 paid out $18,000 in piñon nuts.

4. Early trade was without monetary exchange. A simple hands across the counter transaction prevailed — a good rug for a week's supply of groceries, a kerosene lamp and several yards of velveteen; or four sheep for a saddle, an ax, some rope and a black, wide-rimmed Mallory hat. As refinements in purchases were introduced, tokens (called secos) were used as legal tender. Usually made of a brass alloy (some were leather), these

chips were issued in various denominations and were often stamped with the trader's name, implying their value was only redeemable at his post. Secos were discontinued in 1935. In the modern era, monetary exchange is the basic transaction, although Les Wilson at Two Grey Hills reports that he still "trades" occasionally with several long-time customers.

5. Even in the modern era, the trader is not allowed to own the land that his post is situated upon. The arrangement with the Navajo tribe is a periodic lease renewal policy, and if the trader decides to vacate, or the lease is revoked, the investment of buildings and inventory can only be sold to another trader. After World War II, the tribe instituted a proceeds lease arrangement, whereby the trader is taxed on a percentage of his monthly sales. The three exceptions to early, private ownership on the reservation were Hubbell's homestead at Ganado, Sam Day's homestead at St. Michaels (*see Additional Notes 36, 38 below*) and Wide Ruins (*see Chapter 10*).

6. The hogan (hoghan) is the basic Navajo dwelling. Constructed of variable combinations of logs, brush, mud and rock, the unit can be one of two forms — conical or the six-sided dome shape. Guest hogans at trading posts began to appear around the turn of the century. They were primarily erected to accommodate those Indians who had to travel a great distance to trade, or who were stranded by bad weather. At Shonto, four guest hogans were built in 1930 in hopes of enticing tourists to "lay over" during their tours of the Indian country (see title page sketch). These shelters may have been the primitive prototype of the modern-day motel. An interesting note to the Shonto hogans was their use in a 1932 Universal Pictures movie entitled *Laughing Boy*. This on-location motion picture was undoubtedly the first filmed on the reservation and preceded the classic John Ford Western *Stagecoach*, filmed in nearby Monument Valley, by six years.

The Craft

7. Foote and Schackel (1986, p.21) report that Pueblo men of this period were the principal weavers in the household.

8. The *Chief Blanket* is somewhat controversial. Some writers have clouded its origin and intent by stating that Navajos did not have chiefs, and that the blanket was woven principally as a highly prized barter item for chiefs of other Indian tribes — hence its name. This is erroneous. The fact remains that the Navajos did recognize chiefs and that various headsmen are shown in photographs wearing the fabric. It was not, however, a symbol of rank or leadership and anyone could wear them. Because the blanket represented a superior weave and possessed design appeal, it became an expensive item to own, and was usually only affordable by the more influential and wealthy — "the chiefs" (Martin Link, personal communication, 1987). The *Chief Blanket* evolved through four recognized phases of development depending upon the variable uses of dyes and patterns (Houlihan and others, 1987, p. 53; Kaufman and Selser, 1985, p. 27-33).

9. Navajo weavers had access to bayeta early in the 1800s, but only in rare quantity. Amsden (1934, p. 142n) refers to the first half of the 19th century as the "bayeta period". The natural source of the color red used in bayeta was from dyes called lac and cochineal, which were produced from the powdered remains of Mexican cactus beetles.

10. The period between 1880-1890 became known as the era of the "eyedazzlers". With the analine-dyed Germantown yarns to work with, the weavers now possessed a full spectrum of vibrant colors. The designs remained basically Mexican-Saltillo diamond motifs, which consisted of multiple outlines and zigzags that often resulted in an explosion of combating colors. Many examples were woven with decorative fringe threads

at the top and bottom. Today, the "eyedazzler" is much in demand as a collector's item.

11. James (1934) credits a Fort Defiance trader named Ben Hyatt with introducing aniline dyes to the reservation in 1878. The term "aniline", which denotes a coal-tar based colorant, was the prominent early synthetic dye in common use on the reservation during the last decades of the 19th century.

12. The concept of the bordered rug may have been introduced to weavers as early as the Bosque Redondo days. During their confinement, the Navajos were supplied with thousands of Hispanic-woven (Rio Grande) blankets for wearing apparel. These items included modifications of old Mexican-Saltillo designs, some of which may have included borders (Kaufman and Selser, 1985, p.53). Amsden (1934, p.170) states that the first bordered rug dates from 1873.

13. The teaming of Hubbell and the Fred Harvey Company proved to be a lucrative association, and by the turn of the century, Hubbell undoubtedly was one of the leading rug dealers in America. In the year 1902 alone, Hubbell, negotiating through Harvey's representative buyer, Herman Schweizer, sold $60,000 worth of rugs (Kaufman and Selser, 1985).

14. Moore also experimented with machine-spun wool and commercially dyed yarns (Bulow, 1986).

15. Three areas in the regional style are currently breaking down. The *Chinle* and *Lukachukai Yei* rugs are losing their identities, mainly because of a lack of a trader stimuli. Similarly, the area denoted as Western Reservation, generally regarded as the birthplace of the *Storm Pattern* rug, is no longer the dominant weaving center for this style piece. In a counter move, a vegetal-dyed (commercial yarn), raised outline-style rug with *Teec Nos Pos* designs (called the *New Lands*), is slowly gaining popularity as a possible new regional style (*see Chapter 12*).

16. Some clarification is necessary on the definition of processed wool and commercial yarn, as both terms are being bantered about almost interchangeably. Processed wool, or "roving", as it is sometimes called, is raw wool that has been plant- cleaned and carded into grades of undyed fibers that are packaged into 25-pound bales. Weavers can purchase the wool in varying quantities, spin it, and either vegetal or synthetic dye the product to their liking.

Commercial yarn is already processed wool that has been spun into various ply grades (usually in one-ply skeins). In most instances, it has already been synthetically dyed, either in bright colors or soft pastel hues that resemble the vegetal tones, or uncolored skeins can be vegetal dyed with traditional plant recipes. In some instances, a weaver will purchase lighter shades of colored yarn and overdye it with a concoction of their own to create an entirely new tone. Because commercial yarns are already spun, ply-measured and obtainable in a multiple range of colors, it is this time-saving product that is in principal use in the craft today.

17. Because of the higher prices being commanded (and received) by weavers, many are returning to the loom, including some elderly women. Children are also being trained at an early age, and teenage weavers in some locales are turning out excellent pieces. Several traders also report that men are beginning to submit rugs for sale. Bruce Burnham (personal communication, 1987) of Sanders, Arizona, suspects that some men may have been "closet weavers" for a number of years, but sold their products under their wife's name because it wasn't seen as a manly activity. Now that the craft is economically attractive and has been elevated to a true art form, this is no

longer the situation. Burnham also reports that some best-of-show weavers have recently been men, and in producing the raised outline textile (in the Sanders area), outnumber the women.

18. Some traders refer to this practice as "hogan-hopping".

Chapter 2
From Sheep To Rug

19. Reference to the color black as a natural wool tone is in error. In most cases it is dyed synthetically to further inhance its tone, because natural shorn black wool is not a true, solid black.

20. The preparation of the warp thread is done during the spinning process. In almost all cases the threads are natural wool — the one exception being the prevalent use of cotton warp in the small table-top covers of the *Gallup Throw*.

21. Amsden (1934) outlined nine types of Navajo weaves: plain weave, double weave, two-faced weave and six twill weaves. The tapestry technique is employed in all of these types. It is the arrangement of the heddles that produces the variants. The so-called "wedge weave" might be considered the one exception, whereby the basic horizontal attitude of the warp is altered. Though rarely practiced in modern time, the "wedge weave" (called "pulled warp" by Amsden), enjoyed popularity during the 1880s-1890s. The principal approach was the stretching of the warp at oblique angles to allow the weft to conform to desired patterns, which were usually set in diagonal, interlocking zigzags. Some writings referred to this style as "lightning weave".

22. Considering those fabrics that are well woven, the finely constructed commercial yarns are running from $200-$300 a square foot; vegetal dyes $250-$350 a square foot; and the natural wool products upwards of $400 a square foot.

23. One of the more interesting facets of the trading post system that has gone unreported, is that traders often trade among themselves. This has added significantly to the circulation of rug styles throughout the reservation.

Chapter 3
Shiprock

24. Also located within the Shiprock weaving area, particularly around the trading posts of Cove and Red Rock, are weavers who produce excellent Sandpainting rugs.

Chapter 5
Teec Nos Pos

25. Black Horse (called Be-sho-she in Navajo) a Beautiful Mountain area clan chief, whose dislike for the white man prompted defiant behavior, was responsible for a near rebellion in 1913 that necessitated quelling by U.S. Army troops from Fort Bliss, Texas (McKibben, 1954). The incident which spawned the uprising was the arrest of several clan members involved in plural marriages.

Chapter 6
Crystal

26. Simpson (1850, p.78)

27. The Crystal Trading Post was closed in the fall of 1988. Mail service is now directed through Navajo, New Mexico.

28. Record Group 75, No. 11520 (1884). National Archives, Washington, D.C.

29. When Charlie Newcomb first began trading at Crystal in 1922, a considerable amount of "Moore wool" was still on hand. It was Newcomb's suppo-

sition that the machine-processed fiber was milled somewhere in Wisconsin (McNitt, 1962, p.254n).

Assisted by his wife, Moore also experimented with synthetic dyes, and they reportedly spent long hours in their kitchen preparing dyed wool for area weavers. Don Jensen transmitted to the author (written communication, February 3, 1975) that shortly after he purchased the post, Moore's daughter paid a visit to Crystal. It was her recounting that her parents died prematurely in Kansas in 1923 from what she attributed to "lead poisoning" from prolonged inhaling of dyebath fumes in galvanized pails.

30. Moore's sudden departure from Crystal was clouded with controversy. A local welfare scandal involving heating oil supplies, in which he was not personally involved, was embarrassing to the point of forcing him to leave.

31. Don Jensen, who traded at Crystal between 1944 and 1981, is responsible for the development of the modern Crystal rug. Jensen credits a frequent visitor, a Dr. Hunt, professor at Stanford University and part-time collector and buyer for *Sunset Magazine*, for encouraging a return to Classic Period stripes and bands constructed with vegetal dyes on a borderless format. Hunt's inspiration was the earlier successes at Chinle and Wide Ruins in the adoption of this style. Jensen further elaborates that there was some minor vegetal dyeing being attempted in the area a few years prior to his residency, and that a weaver named Desbah Nez is credited with being the first Crystal weaver to utilize plant concoctions in wool colors.

32. The "wavy-line" technique is a distinct Crystal trait and signature creation. Don Jensen reports that the first rug he saw with this undulating feature was by Imelda Nez in 1944. Jensen says that the technique caught on quickly, but that its ultimate popularity prompted weavers to ask a higher price for rugs that incorporated the feature.

Chapter 7
Two Grey Hills

33. Sometimes spelled Two Gray Hills. A post office, called Crozier, New Mexico, existed on the post grounds between 1903-1919.

34. Carded black and white = gray; carded brown and white = tan and beige.

Chapter 8
Chinle

35. Spelled Chin Lee prior to 1941, and at times, Chinlee. It roughly translates to, "it flows from the canyon", or "at the mouth of the canyon".

36. Clinton Neal Cotton (1859-1936), a one-time partner with Hubbell at Ganado and Chinle, is an individual often overlooked in the historical development of Navajo weaving. A native of Ohio, he headed west as a telegraph operator. While working for the Atlantic and Pacific Railroad at Albuquerque and at Fort Wingate, he became friends with Juan Lorenzo Hubbell, and a lifelong business association ensued.

Cotton and Hubbell entered into a partnership in 1884 when the former bought a half interest in the trading post at Ganado. Williams (1989) states that Cotton actually purchased the post from Hubbell a year later and held a license on its operation until at least 1902. This "ownership" was probably a *quasi* arrangement, necessitated by Hubbell's long absences in St. John's, where he served as sheriff of Apache County, Arizona.

When Hubbell homesteaded the original 160 acres in 1878, the land lay outside the Navajo Reservation, and he was not required to secure a license to trade. When the boundary line was redrawn and enlarged by the Executive Order on January 6, 1880, the facility fell within the confines of the reservation and under law required a license.

The Hubbell-Cotton partnership operated the post for a period of time without a license which prompted considerable haggling with government officials. Under threats of the property being razed, and considering Hubbell's frequent absences during this time, the responsibility, no doubt, fell on Cotton to secure a license, which was ultimately dated November 22, 1887 (Williams, 1989). By the issuance of the license to Cotton, it implied his sole ownership, but it is highly doubtful that Hubbell would have completely dissolved all of his holdings at Ganado. The arrangement of this "sale" was probably more of a convenience between two understanding partners than an actual transaction. Difficulties over the Ganado licensing probably played a role in the denying of a license that Cotton and Hubbell sought for trading at Chinle in 1885 (see page 58). The matter of Hubbell's homestead was finally resolved on July 28, 1917, when he was finally issued a formal deed to the property — nearly 40 years after establishing his residency.

The date of Hubbell's "repurchase" of the Ganado post from Cotton is unknown, but it was probably sometime shortly after the turn of the century. In the interim, Cotton had disengaged himself from active trading, left the reservation, moved to Gallup, New Mexico, and began a wholesale business that supplied goods to the Navajo, Hopi and Zuni reservations. The C. N. Cotton Company, incorporated in 1903, grew into a highly successful enterprise. An integral part of the operation was the wholesaling of Navajo rugs. Cotton published the first mail-order catalogue for rugs, including the first use of color photographs. He developed a large clientele in Eastern markets and over a three-decade period, sold thousands of rugs, which in turn, greatly benefited the weaving industry.

Cotton served as mayor of Gallup during 1916-1918 and was the first president of the McKinley County Bank. He was highly regarded, not only by the citizens of Gallup, but also by his Indian neighbors, and the people of western New Mexico and eastern Arizona. His contributions to Navajo weaving place him alongside the likes of Hubbell and Moore as one of the most influential servants of the craft.

37. This site later served as the location for the first Post Office building in Chinle. The hillock is situated directly across the main road (north) from the Catholic Church.

38. Sam Day is credited with the discovery of Massacre Cave and other significant archaeological findings in Canyon de Chelly in 1904. His son, Charles, was later appointed the first custodian (pre-National Park Service management) in protecting artifacts of the canyon. Day, who led a varied and colorful life, was already of advanced age when licensed to trade. He was a lanky six-footer who was born in Canton, Ohio, in 1845. A drifter of sorts, he had briefly studied civil engineering in Newark, New Jersey, before joining the Union Army during the Civil War. After his enlistment, he headed west to the gold fields of South Dakota, found a young woman (Anna P. Burnbridge, who married him in Iowa) and eventually settled in Colorado for a short time. Hired as a surveyor for the federal government, Day and his family moved to Arizona in the early 1880s, where he homesteaded, and spent several years delineating the eastern and southern boundaries of the Navajo Reservation (Harrison and Spears, 1987).

Following his trading days at Chinle, Day retired to his homestead at Cienega Amarilla, Spanish for "Yellow Marsh." He had established the property prior to its inclusion within the boundaries of the reservation. In later years he donated the land to the Catholic Church (Franciscan O.F.M. Order) for use as a hospital and school for Indian children; it was renamed St. Michaels. Located a short distance west of present-day Window Rock, Arizona, the place is now a designated historic site.

39. Raised in Boston, Mary Cabot Wheelwright was a scholar of world comparative religions. She arrived in the Southwest in 1918 and became enamored with Navajo traditions. She established a friendship with the famous medicine man, Hosteen Klah of Newcomb, New Mexico, and together in 1937 they founded the House of Navajo Religion in Santa Fe. It later evolved to become the Wheelwright Museum of the American Indian. Miss Wheelwright died in 1948.

Chapter 9
Ganado

40. The Crary site, the first trading post after Fort Defiance, is thought to have been located on Pueblo Colorado Wash near Ganado Lake, three miles northeast of the present Hubbell post. The Leonard location is the original ground of Hubbell's later operation.

McNitt (1962, p.201n) points out some discrepancies in the chronology of events that established the Hubbell post. Late in life, Hubbell (1930) states that he purchased his holdings in 1876 from a man named "Williams." In the National Archives (Record Group 75), records show that Lorenzo was still employed as a clerk at Fort Defiance during the summer and fall of 1876, and it seems unlikely that his trading days could have started at that time. The "Williams" that Hubbell was referring to may have been Perry H. Williams, who on March 31, 1877, was licensed to trade at Washington Pass. It could also have been George M. "Barney" Williams, who was mentioned by Bourke (1884) as trading on Pueblo Colorado Wash in 1881. [This "Williams" more than likely operated at the old Crary location.]

Four years after Lorenzo's death, Eckel (1934) wrote that the founding sequence of Hubbell Trading Post started with Charles Crary, who sold to Leonard in 1875, who in turn, sold to Hubbell the following year (1876). Since Eckel was Hubbell's granddaughter, many historians have accepted her writings as fact. From the documented presence of Leonard during 1876-1878, however, logical assumption is to place Hubbell at Ganado in late 1876, possibly clerking for Leonard, then buying him out in 1878. Hubbell later applied for and was granted a homestead of 160 acres at the site. This was before the area was included within the expanded boundaries of the reservation before 1880.

41. Hubbell was born in 1853 at Pajarito, New Mexico, the son of a Connecticut Yankee who had gone to New Mexico as a soldier and married into a Spanish family. Mostly self-educated, he became familiar with the life, ways and language of the Navajos while traveling about the Southwest as a young man and serving as a clerk and a Spanish interpreter.

Hubbell — "Old Mexican" or "Double Glasses" to the Navajos, was not only their merchant, but also their guide and teacher in understanding the ways of the white man. He was a trusted friend who translated and wrote letters, settled family quarrels, explained government policy and helped the sick. His commitment to excellence and craftmanship resulted in an enduring influence on Navajo weaving. Beyond question, he was the foremost Navajo trader of his time.

Hubbell's career as a trader spanned critical years for the Navajos. He came to Ganado when the Indians were trying to adjust to reservation life following their confinement at Fort Sumner, New Mexico. More than any other white man, he was often their spokesman and contact with the outside world. Though a Roman Catholic, Hubbell persuaded the Presbyterian Board of Foreign Missions to choose nearby Ganado for a mission site and while the mission was being built, took the first missionaries into his home for a year.

42. The succession of traders following Southwest Parks and Monuments Association management include: Bill Young (1967-1979), Al Grieves (1979-1982) and Bill Malone (1982-present).

Chapter 10
Wide Ruins

43. Following John Rieffer's death, the Wide Ruins post was closed in 1982. The store later burned and the remaining complex has now been razed.

44. Prior to 1880, the Wide Ruins area was not part of the Navajo Reservation, therefore, early merchants (not requiring licenses) cannot be traced through government records.

45. Subsequent excavations by the National Geographic Society dates the erection of Kinteel sometime between 1265-1285 A.D.

46. Sallie (Lippincott) Wagner reported to the author that during their stay in California, they sold out to a man named Carl Hine in 1942, but reacquired the property two years later by repossession.

47. Sallie (Lippincott) Wagner reported that when they began trading at Wide Ruins in 1938, the weaving effort was in a terrible state. The main products were gaudy, poorly woven pillow-top covers that were sold in curio stands along U.S. Highway 66.

48. In some rug descriptions, the term "Lippincott pink" is occasionally used. This particular hue, reports Sallie (Lippincott) Wagner, was obtained from the red lichen that grew on nearby oak shrubs.

Chapter 11
Burnt Water

49. The Burnt Water (spelled *Burntwater* in the rug type) Trading Post was closed in 1983.

50. Jacobs also credits Laura Murphy, another expert area weaver, with early contributions to the *Burntwater* rug.

51. Bruce Burnham is initiating experiments by issuing uncolored commercial yarn to area weavers to be native plant dyed with home recipes.

Chapter 12
New Lands

52. The raised outline weave is referred to by weavers as *hoshtodi*, which translates in visual meaning to the variegated feathers of the Bull Bat owl.
Kent (1981, p.20) questions the time and origin of the raised outline technique that is attributed to Ned Hatathi and the Coal Mine Mesa weavers in 1950. She cites a raised outline textile, now in collection at the Museum of Northern Arizona in Flagstaff, which was woven at Ganado in 1934. This evidence predates the guild project by sixteen years.

53. Kent (1981, p.20) describes the raised outline technique as:

> ...basically a plain weave tapestry, but along the edges of two figures, where wefts meet and turn back on themselves, there appears to be a ridge. This is what gives the weave its name. The effect is obtained by inserting a weft of one color, followed by a weft of another color in the next shed. Both wefts move in the same direction — say from right to left. When they reach the edge of the figure they are making, each passes over two warps, instead of the usual one. It is these long floats that appear to be raised. *(Reproduced from* The Plateau Quarterly, *courtesy of Museum of Northern Arizona.)*

54. Between 1878 and 1886 the Navajo Reservation was enlarged by five land additions. One of these, the Navajo-Hopi Joint Use Area, was created by an Executive Order signed by President Chester A. Arthur on December 16, 1882. This action, which has plagued northern Arizona for over a cen-

tury, carved out two and a half million acres (for sharing with the Navajo) from what the Hopi tribe believed to be their traditional land. In subsequent years, a clash of cultures and wills prevailed over the land sharing, resulting in some violence, numerous court actions and federal suits. A bitter solution was reached in 1974 when the U.S. Congress voted 90,000 acres of disputed land to be turned back exclusively to the Hopis. A Navajo-Hopi Joint Land Commission was ultimately created to oversee and manage a peaceful transition. Over 1,200 Navajo families have now been relocated from the contested area; more are destined to follow. Iverson (1988) points out that this dispute has been settled equitably and that Hopis, although smaller in numbers, are residing on Navajo property, and they are also subject to relocation.

55. Bruce Burnham (personal communication, 1998) reported that the land acquisition was in excess of one million acres centered approximately 15 miles southeast of Sanders, Arizona. Residences have already been constructed, and a New Lands Chapter has been established.

Chapter 13
Western Reservation

56. The Red Lake Trading Post closed in the spring of 1987, and a new general (convenience) store, no longer in the trading business, is located one-half mile to the west.

57. Letter communication: Paul Babbitt, Jr., Babbitt Brothers Trading Company, Flagstaff, Arizona (November 23, 1973).

58. The Western Reservation is also noted for two specialty type weaves: Pictorials (particularly Bird rugs) are prevalent around The Gap trading area, and Shonto is known for its Saddle Blankets.

59. The four sacred mountains of Navajo mythology are: East — *Sisnaajini* (Sierra Blanca, Colorado); West — *Doko'ooaliid* (San Francisco Peak, Arizona); North — *Dibentsaa* (Mount Hesperus, Colorado); and South — *Tsoodzil* (Mount Taylor, New Mexico).

APPENDIX I

Rules in Buying a Navajo Rug

Remember, a Navajo rug is not perfect; if it were, it would look like a machine-made fabric and thus lose the charm of being handmade. Small flaws are acceptable only if they do not detract from the overall presentation of the fabric.

Always open the rug to full width and length. Smooth out all the wrinkles, folds and corners. The rug should not curl up and should be even in form. Look at both sides, get the full visual impact of the design.

Check the weave. Is it tight? Is the design uniform and even from one end to the other? The ends and borders should be straight and the corners properly tied off. Make sure there are no warp threads exposed.

Feel the smoothness of the rug. Is the wool texture the same throughout the fabric? Watch for heavy lumping; likewise, thinly spaced areas.

Watch for color uniformity. Since only a small amount of yarn can be dyed at one time, a weaver may become careless with her dyebath and variations may emerge. In the natural white tones, watch for dirty, gray castes, as well as streaks of other cardings. Also whitening agents, such as powder and chalk, may be used to conceal dirty wool or yarn.

Consider the overall motif. Does it fulfill your purpose of purchase? Will it fit into your scheme of home decorating? Will it hang on the wall, or be placed on the floor?

Buy it! If the appeal is aesthetically right, the size is right and the price is right. Fine Navajo rugs are a good investment. The good rugs sell quickly and do not linger on the racks. The one you had your eye on today may be gone tomorrow.

Consult and buy from quality dealers. Outlets with good reputations cannot afford to deal in rugs with the unfavorable characteristics and practices outlined here.

Beware of Mexican imitations. Excellent replicas of Navajo designs are sometimes misrepresented and the unsuspecting buyer can be easily misled. The principle keys in **recognizing** a Mexican rug are: (1) examine for multiple warps along the sides, (2) knotted warps along the top and bottom and (3) a coarse, loosely woven product. **Exercise caution** with seemingly "good deal" prices.

APPENDIX II

Care of a Navajo Rug

When a rug is placed on the floor, **use** a foam mat beneath.

Rotate the sides of the rug and reverse the ends occasionally. This will allow for uniform wear and mellowing of colors. When hung on a wall, a rug is usually in more direct sunlight, and rotation should be more frequent. Normal vacuum cleaning is sufficient.

Never "shake out" a rug; the snapping action my loosen the end cords, causing warp and weft threads to unravel.

Never wash the rug. If small spots occur, commercial removers will usually suffice. If a major cleaning is necessary, consult a reputable rug dealer for recommendations of a dry cleaner who specializes in rug care.

If water is spilled on a rug, blot it **immediately** to minimize the running of colors. Improperly set colorants (both vegetal and commercial), when combined with water can literally destroy the visual portrait of a rug. The color red is the hardest to clean.

Navajo rugs should **always** be de-mothed, whether they are in use or not.

In wall hangings, remember to treat both sides. If a rug is to be stored for an indefinite period, always **roll** it; folding may cause crimping of the threads, resulting in permanent creases.

Cedar-lined chests are **recommended** as safe, suitable storage containers.

In some rugs, a minor curling effect may occur along the ends and corners. Simply **untie** the end cords, gently smooth out the curled surface and re-tie the end cords.

Bibliography
1882-1991

Adair, John. *The Navajo and Pueblo Silversmiths*. Norman: University of Oklahoma Press, 1944.

Amsden, Charles Avery. *Navajo Weaving, Its Technic [sic] and History*. Santa Barbara: Fine Arts Press 1934.

Bahti, Tom. *Introduction To Southwestern Indian Arts and Crafts*. Flagstaff: K.C. Publications, 1966.

Bennett, Nöel and Tina Bighorse. *Working with the Wool*. Flagstaff: Northland Press, 1971.

——. *The Weaver's Pathway*. Flagstaff: Northland Press, 1974.

Bourke, John J. *The Snake-Dance of the Moquis of Arizona*. London: Sampson, Low, Marstan, Seale & Rivington, 1884.

Bryan, Nonabah and Stella Young. *Native Navajo Dyes*. Washington: U.S. Department of the Interior, 1940.

Bulow, Ernie. (Introduction), *The Navajo*. Albuquerque: Avanyu Publishing Company, 1986. (*Reprint*).

Burbank, E. A. *Burbank Among the Indians*. Caldwell: Caxton Printers, 1944.

Coolidge, Dane and Mary Coolidge. *The Navajo Indians*. Boston: Houghton Mifflin Company, 1930.

DeLauer, Marjel. "A Century of Indian Traders and Trading Posts," *Arizona Highways Magazine*. Phoenix: vol. 51, no. 3, 1975.

Dutton, Bertha. *Navajo Weaving Today*. Santa Fe: Museum of New Mexico Press, 1961.

Eckel, LaCharles Goodman. *History of Ganado, Arizona* Flagstaff: Museum of Northern Arizona, vol. 6, no. 10, 1934.

Fontana, Bernard L. "Kit Carson in Arizona," *Arizona Highways Magazine*. Phoenix: v. 64. no. 1, 1988.

Foote, Cheryl J. and Sandra K. Schackel. "Indian Women in New Mexico, 1535-1680," *New Mexico Women, Intercultural Perspectives*. Albuquerque: University of New Mexico Press, 1986.

Getzwiler, Steve. *The Fine Art of Navajo Weaving*. Tucson: Ray Manley Publications, 1984.

Gillmor, Francis and Louisa Wade Wetherill. *Traders to the Navajo*. Albuquerque: University of New Mexico Press, 1952.

Gilpin, Laura. *The Enduring Navajo*. Austin: University of Texas Press, 1971.

Granger, Byrd H., (ed.). *Arizona Place Names*. Tucson: University of Arizona Press, 1960.

Hannum, Alberta. *Spin a Silver Dollar: The Story of a Desert Trading Post*: New York: The Viking Press, 1944.

——. *Paint the Wind*. New York: The Viking Press, 1958.

Harrison, Laura Soullière and Beverly Spears. "Historic Structures Report, Chinle Trading Post and Custodian's Residence, Canyon de Chelly National Monument, Arizona" [*unpublished draft*]. Santa Fe: National Park Service, 1987.

Hegemann, Elizabeth Compton. *Navaho Trading Days*. Albuquerque: University of New Mexico Press, 1963.

Hill, Willard W. "Navajo Trading and Trading Ritual, a Study of Cultural Dynamics," *Southwestern Journal of Anthropology*, v. 4, no. 4. Albuquerque: University of New Mexico Press, 1948.

Hollister, U.S. *The Navajo and his Blanket*: New Mexico: Rio Grande Press, Glorieta, 1972. (*Reprint*).

Hubbell, Lorenzo. "Fifty Years an Indian Trader," *Touring Topics*, v. 22, no. 12.1930.

Houlihan, Patrick, Jerold L. Collins, Sarah Nestor, and Jonathan Batkin. *Harmony by Hand*. Dal Mar: McQuiston & Daughter, Inc., 1987.

Iverson, Peter. "Knowing the Land, Leaving the Land: Navajos, Hopis, and Relocation in the American West," *Montana — The Magazine of Western History*, vol. 38, no.1. Helena: Montana Historical Society, 1988.

James, George Wharton. *Indian Blankets and Their Makers*. Chicago: A.C. McClurg & Company, 1934.

James, H. L. "The Santa Fe Trail," *Guidebook of the Taos, Raton, Spanish Peaks Country*. Socorro: New Mexico Geological Society, 1966.

—. "The History of Fort Wingate," *Guidebook of the Defiance-Zuni-Mt. Taylor Region*. Socorro: New Mexico Geological Society, 1967.

—. "Navajo Rugs, the Regional Style," *Guidebook of Monument Valley and Vicinity, Arizona and Utah*. Socorro: New Mexico Geological Society, 1973.

—."The Romance of Navajo Weaving," *New Mexico Magazine*, v. 52, no. 1. Santa Fe: 1974.

—. *Posts and Rugs: The Story of Navajo Rugs and Their Homes*. Globe: Southwest Parks and Monuments Association, 1974.

Jeffers, Jo. "Hubbell Trading Post National Historic Site," *Arizona Highways Magazine*, v. 43, no. 9: Phoenix: 1967.

Kahlenberg, Mary Hunt and Anthony Berlant. *The Navajo Blanket*: Los Angeles: Praeger Publishing Company, 1972.

Kaufman, Alice and Christopher Selser. *The Navajo Weaving Tradition, 1650 to the Present*: New York: E.P. Dutton, Inc., 1985.

Kent, Kate Peck. *The Story of Navajo Weaving*. Phoenix: Heard Museum, 1961.

—. "From Blanket to Rug: the Evolution of Navajo Weaving After 1880," *The Plateau Quarterly*, v. 52, no. 4: Flagstaff: Museum of Northern Arizona, 1981.

—. *Navajo Weaving: Three Centuries of Change*. Santa Fe: School of American Research Press, 1985.

Kluckhorn, Clyde and Dorothea Leighton. *The Navajo*. Garden City: Doubleday Publishing Company, 1962.

Koeing, Harriet and Seymour H. Koeing. *Navajo Weaving-Navajo Ways*. Katonah: Katonah Gallery, 1986.

Lesch, Alma. *Vegetable Dyeing*. New York: Watson-Guptill Publishing Company: 1970.

Luomala, Katherine. "Navajo Weaving," *El Palacio Quarterly*, v. 80, no. 1. Santa Fe: Museum of New Mexico Press, 1974.

Matthews, Washington."Navajo Weavers," *U.S. Bureau of American Ethnology*, 3rd Annual Report. Washington: 1882.

—. "The Night Chant, A Navajo Ceremony," *Memoirs of The American Museum of Natural History*, v. 6. Washington: 1902.

—. *Navajo Weavers and Silversmiths*. Palmer Lake: 1968 (*Reprint*).

Maxwell, Gilbert S. *Navajo Rugs—Past, Present and Future*. Palm Desert: Best-West Publications, 1963.

McCoy, Ron. "*Naalye he Bahooghan* — Where the Past is the Present," *Arizona Highways Magazine*, v. 63, no. 6. Phoenix: 1987.

McKibben, D.B. "Revolt of the Navaho — 1913," *New Mexico Historical Review*, v. 24, no. 4. Albuquerque: University of New Mexico Press, 1954.

McLuhan, T.C. *Dream Tracks: The Railroad and the American Indian, 1890-1930*. New York: Harry N. Abrams, Inc., 1985.

McNitt, Frank. "Two Gray Hills — America's Costliest Rugs," *New Mexico Magazine*, v. 37, no. 4. Santa Fe: 1959.

—. *The Indian Traders*. Norman: University of Oklahoma Press, 1962.

—, (ed.). *Navajo Expedition*. Norman: University of Oklahoma Press, 1964. *(Reprint)*.

—. *Navajo Wars*. Albuquerque: University of New Mexico Press, 1972.

Mera, H.P. *Navajo Textile Arts*. Santa Fe: New Mexico Laboratory of Anthropology, 1949.

Miller, Marjorie. *Indian Arts and Crafts*. Los Angeles: Nash Publishing Company, 1972.

Mills, George. *Navaho Art and Culture*. Colorado Springs: Taylor Museum Fine Arts Center, 1959.

Moore, J.B. *The Navajo*. Denver: Williamson-Haffner Company, 1911.

Mott, Dorothy Challis. "Don Lorenzo Hubbell of Ganado," *Arizona Historical Review*, v. 4, no.1. Tucson, 1931.

National Park Service. "Hubbell Trading Post National Historic Site"(*Visitor Pamphlet*). Washington: National Park Service, 1986.

Newcomb, Franc Johnson. *Hosteen Klah: Navajo Medicine Man and Sand Painter*. Norman: University of Oklahoma Press, 1964.

—. *Navajo Neighbors*. Norman: University of Oklahoma Press, 1966.

Pearce, T. M., (ed.). *New Mexico Place Names*. Albuquerque: University of New Mexico Press, 1965.

Pendleton, Mary. *Navajo and Hopi Weaving Techniques*. New York: Collier Books, 1974.

Reichard, Gladys A. *Dezba: Woman of the Desert*: New York: J.J. Augustin Company, 1939.

—. *Navajo Shepherd and Weaver*. Glorieta: Rio Grande Press, 1968. *(Reprint)*

—. *Spider Woman*. Glorieta: Rio Grande Press, 1968. *(Reprint)*.

Richardson, Gladwell. *Navajo Trader*. Tucson: University of Arizona Press, 1986.

Rodee, Marian. *Old Navajo Rugs*. Albuquerque: University of New Mexico Press, 1981.

—. *Weaving of the Southwest*. West Chester: Schiffer Publishing, Ltd., 1987.

Schiffer, Nancy. *Navajo Weaving Today*. West Chester: Schiffer Publishing, Ltd.. 1991.

—. *Navajo Arts and Crafts*. West Chester: Schiffer Publishing, Ltd., 1991.

Simpson, James H. *Reconnaissance Expedition into the Navajo Country*, U.S. Senate Document No. 64. Washington: 1850.

Spiegelberg, A. F. "Navajo Blankets," *El Palacio Quarterly*, v. 18, nos. 10, 11. Santa Fe: Museum of New Mexico Press, 1925.

Tanner, Clara Lee, "Modern Navajo Weaving," *Arizona Highways Magazine*, vol. 40, no. 9. Phoenix: 1964.

—. *Southwest Indian Craft Arts*. Tucson: University of Arizona Press, 1968.

Twitchell, Ralph Emerson. *The Leading Facts of New Mexico History*. Albuquerque: Horn & Wallace Publishing Company, 1963.

Underhill, Ruth. *Pueblo Crafts*. Lawrence: Haskell Institute, 1944.

—. *Here Come the Navajo*. Lawrence: Haskell Institute, 1953.

—. *The Navajo*. Norman: University of Oklahoma Press, 1956.

U.S. Federal Trade Commission. *The Trading Post System on the Navajo Reservation*. Washington: U.S. Printing Office, 1973.

Utley, Robert M. "The Reservation Trader in Navajo History," *El Palacio Quarterly*, v. 68, no. 1. Santa Fe: Museum of New Mexico Press, 1961.

Utley, Robert M. and Wilcomb E. Washburn. "American Heritage of the Indian Wars," *American Heritage*: New York, 1977.

Van Valkenburgh, Richard F. *A Short History of the Navajo People.* New York: Garland Publications, 1974.

Watson, Editha L. "Navajo Rugs," *Arizona Highways Magazine*, v. 33, no. 8. Phoenix: 1957.

—. "Navajo History: A 3,000-Year Sketch," *Guidebook of Monument Valley and Vicinity, Arizona and Utah.* Socorro: New Mexico Geological Society, 1973.

Wheat, Joe Ben. "Three Centuries of Navajo Weaving," *Arizona Highways Magazine*, v. 50, no. 7. Phoenix: 1974.

—. "Early Navajo Weaving," *The Plateau Quarterly*, v. 52, no. 4. Flagstaff: Museum of Northern Arizona, 1981.

Whiteford, Andrew Hunter. *North American Indian Arts.* New York: Western Publishing Company, 1970.

Williams, Lester L. *C. N. Cotton and His Navajo Blankets.* Albuquerque: Avanyu Publishing Inc., 1989.

Pertinent titles issued by the Laboratory of Anthropology (Technological Series), Santa Fe, New Mexico:

Bulletin No. 3 — *Navajo Blankets of the Classic Period* (1938)
Bulletin No. 5 — *The Slave Blanket* (1938)
Bulletin No. 6 — *Pictorial Blankets* (1938)
Bulletin No. 9 — *Wedge Weave Blankets* (1939)
Bulletin No. 12 — *The Zoning Treatment in Navajo Blanket Design* (1940)
Bulletin No. 13 — *The Chinlee Rug* (1942)
Bulletin No. 14 — *Navajo Twilled Weaving* (1943)
Bulletin No. 15 — *Navajo Woven Dresses* (1943)
Bulletin No. 16 — *Cloth Strip Blankets of the Navajo* (1945)

INDEX